The Inn Country USA Cookbook

Also from Berkshire House Publishers

The Innkeepers Collection Cookbook
C. Vincent Shortt

Country Inns and Back Roads Cookbook
Linda Glick Conway

The Kripalu Cookbook: Gourmet Vegetarian Recipes
Atma Jo Ann Levitt

The Red Lion Inn Cookbook
Suzi Forbes Chase

Apple Orchard Cookbook
Janet M. Christensen and Betty Bergman Levin

Best Recipes of Berkshire Chefs
Miriam Jacobs

The Inn Country USA Cookbook

C. Vincent Shortt

Berkshire House Publishers
Stockbridge, Massachusetts

The Inn Country USA Cookbook
Copyright © 1995 by Berkshire House Publishers

Interior photographs and photography editing by Craig Hammell

Edited by Constance Lee Oxley
Cover design by Pamela Meier
Text design by Catharyn Tivy
Production services by Ripinsky & Company

Library of Congress Cataloging-in-Publication Data
Shortt, C. Vincent, 1947-
The Inn country USA cookbook / C. Vincent Shortt.
    p.   cm.
"As featured on the public television series 'Inn Country USA.'"
Includes index.
ISBN 0-936399-70-8
1. Cookery, American. 2. Hotels—United States—Guidebooks.
I. Inn country USA. II. Title.
TX715.S55886   1995
641.5—dc20   95-13643
                                        CIP

ISBN 0-936399-70-8

10 9 8 7 6 5 4 3 2 1

*This book is dedicated to you. You have made all of
this possible. On behalf of the dozens of production staff who
make our television and print materials possible,
thank you for your thoughtful letters of encouragement and
your enthusiasm for our products.*

*As this world of ours grows smaller and becomes
forever bound up in the ribbon of electronic impulses, your
power and your voice, your feedback and your
comments, and your first-hand suggestions about the little
inn at the end of the road less traveled are always
welcome. In fact, we cherish them. I look forward to
meeting you along the way.*

Contents

Acknowledgment

This book could not have been created without the television series of the same name. To the talented people who make public television possible in the United States, thank you. To the kind and generous viewers and readers who have made our earlier books and television programs successful, thank you.

To the keepers of the inn who get up earlier, stay up later, work harder, try harder, and laugh harder than any other group of people on the face of the earth, thank you.

Without the following folks, this book would not exist—many thanks to my colleague, Chuck McConnell; my bottomless well of secretarial patience, Judy Emminizer; my editor, Constance Oxley; my indefatigable postmaster, Chuck Beres; my writing partners, Russ, Travis, and Sweetie Lee; and finally, I would like to thank my best buddy (and wife) Ann for teaching me the proper use of the two most important ingredients in the kitchen…love and a sense of humor.

C.V.S.

This cookbook is the culmination of a 25-year "love affair" with inns. After producing two inn theme television series and writing three books related to inns and innkeepers, I find myself even more intrigued than ever with the people who invest their lives, their fortunes, and their hearts serving others as keepers of the inn.

Upon reflection of what makes inns and innkeepers so compelling, two reasons come to mind. First, it is the unique distinction of country inns and bed & breakfasts that no two are alike. They are different in every possible way: size, age, theme, personality, location, food. The intrepid inngoer inevitably grows to relish and savor each of these differences. In fact, somewhere along the way to appreciating the differences among inns, I hit upon the other reason. The one common thread that winds its way through the very fabric of this industry and is the basis of all successful inns is that they all serve the same thing—you, me, us.

When we select the inns for our television series, "Inn Country USA," we earnestly strive to celebrate their differences. Nowhere is the difference between an inn in Eureka, California, and an inn on a barrier island off the Georgia coast more apparent than in the fresh, local ingredients that each inn selects to prepare for their guests. When we began collecting recipes from the private files of innkeepers for our previous cookbook, *The Innkeepers Collection Cookbook* (Berkshire House Publishers, 1994), we quickly discovered that our viewers were our readers and our readers wanted more!

With pleasure and pride, here is the most comprehensive collection of recipes ever assembled from a television series dedicated to country inns and bed & breakfasts. Enjoy!

✳

CHAPTER 1

Breakfast & Brunch

Fantastic Pumpkin Pancakes

4 to 6 eggs
1/2 cup canned plain pumpkin
1/2 tablespoon brown sugar
1/2 tablespoon ground nutmeg
1/2 tablespoon ground cinnamon
1 1/2 to 2 cups packaged baking mix
4 cups buttermilk
Pure maple syrup
Blackberry jelly

The Hidden Inn

Imagine getting up every morning and preparing breakfast for 6 or 10 or 12 of your best friends — that is what Ray and Barbara Lonick cheerfully do every morning. They have found that some of their most imaginative and tasty recipes are also the most straight forward to prepare. These *Fantastic Pumpkin Pancakes* have a consistently tasty result, and all of your breakfast guests, whether they number 2 or 20, will love them!

In a large bowl, beat together the eggs, pumpkin, sugar, and spices until well blended. Add the baking mix, 1/2 cup at a time. While continuing to mix, pour in the buttermilk, a little at a time, and beat until smooth. (The batter should not be too thick.) Set the batter aside for 10 to 15 minutes. Stir the batter again and add more milk if too thick.

In a lightly greased hot skillet, ladle the batter and turn the pancake when bubbles appear. As the pancakes are cooked, place on a platter and hold in a warm oven. Serve with the syrup or blackberry jelly.

YIELD: 8 TO 10 SERVINGS

THE HIDDEN INN
ORANGE, VIRGINIA

German Apple Pancakes

4 large eggs
3 tablespoons granulated sugar
1/2 teaspoon baking soda
1/2 cup milk
1/2 cup packaged low-fat baking mix
1/4 cup golden raisins soaked overnight in 1/2 cup cranberry juice
1/3 cup apple liqueur

4 teaspoons vegetable shortening
1 large apple, peeled, quartered, and very thinly sliced
4 to 6 tablespoons vegetable shortening
12 to 18 kiwifruit slices
4 to 6 fresh strawberries, rinsed
Edible flower blossoms
Cinnamon-sugar mixture

In a blender or food processor, blend together the eggs, sugar, baking soda, milk, and baking mix. Drain the raisins and place in a large bowl. Pour the liqueur over the raisins and add the batter.

In an omelette pan, melt the 4 teaspoons shortening on high heat and ladle 2/3 cup of the batter into the pan. Immediately reduce heat to low and spread 6 apple slices on top of the batter. Cover with a second 2/3 cup of batter and cook for 20 minutes on the first side.

Raise heat to high, lift up the pancake, and melt 1 tablespoon of the shortening. Flip the pancake and cook for 5 minutes on the second side or until golden brown. Place in a warm oven and repeat the procedure for the remaining batter.

Garnish each serving with 3 kiwifruit slices, 1 strawberry, and the flowers. Sprinkle with the cinnamon-sugar mixture and serve immediately.

YIELD: 4 TO 6 SERVINGS

ROSE INN
ITHACA, NEW YORK

Dutch Babies (Puffed Oven-Baked Pancakes)

6 tablespoons unsalted butter
6 eggs
1 1/2 cups milk
1 1/2 cups all-purpose flour
1 1/2 teaspoons pure almond extract
3 teaspoons grated lemon peel
Confectioners' sugar
Lemon wedges

The Spencer House

You will see a lot of creative restoration work along the innkeeping trail, but you must see what a well-traveled, retired airline pilot, his hammered copper cookware-importing wife, and wine aficionada daughter have all put their hearts and spirits into—The Spencer House, in the heart of "The Haight."

Preheat oven to 475° F. Place 1 tablespoon of the butter in each of six 4-inch ovenproof ramekins and heat in the oven until the butter is melted. Meanwhile, in a blender or food processor, beat the eggs until light and frothy. Transfer the egg mixture to a large bowl and gradually beat in the milk, then the flour, until the batter is smooth. Stir in the almond extract and lemon zest.

Pour approximately 2/3 cup batter into each ramekin of hot butter and bake for 12 minutes or until puffed and golden. Sprinkle with the confectioners' sugar and squeeze lemon juice over the top. Serve immediately.

YIELD: 6 SERVINGS

The Spencer House
San Francisco, California

Pear Pancakes

6 eggs
1 cup whole milk
1 cup all-purpose flour
4 tablespoons melted butter
$1/2$ teaspoon pure almond extract
2 teaspoons grated lemon peel
3 large baking pears, peeled
2 tablespoons confectioners' sugar
3 tablespoons fresh lemon juice
Confectioners' sugar
Fresh berries or fruit, rinsed

In a medium-sized bowl, beat together the eggs and milk. Stir in the flour. While continuing to beat, add the butter. Stir in the almond extract and lemon zest. Halve, core, and slice the pears. In a large bowl, mix together the 2 tablespoons sugar and lemon juice and toss the sliced pears in the mixture.

Preheat oven to 425° F. In each of six au gratin dishes, layer half of a pear (5 to 6 slices into each dish). Pour $1/2$ cup of the batter over the pears and bake for 20 minutes. Sprinkle with the sugar and berries. Serve immediately.

YIELD: 6 SERVINGS

OLD MONTEREY INN
MONTEREY, CALIFORNIA

Potato Pancakes

2 large Idaho potatoes, peeled and shredded
2 tablespoons diced onions
2 tablespoons chopped fresh chives
6 tablespoons shredded cheddar cheese
2 eggs, beaten
2 tablespoons all-purpose flour
2 teaspoons fresh lemon juice
1/8 teaspoon freshly ground white pepper
2 tablespoons vegetable oil

In a medium-sized bowl, combine the first eight ingredients and mix together well. With hands, squeeze excess liquid from the mixture and form desired-size pancakes.

Heat a large skillet until a water drop sizzles across it. Add the oil and the formed pancake. Cook on each side for 3 minutes or until golden brown. Repeat the procedure with remaining pancakes (1 large or 2 small pancakes per serving). Serve immediately.

YIELD: 4 SERVINGS

PROSPECT HILL PLANTATION INN
TREVILIANS, VIRGINIA

Raised Waffles

³/₄ cup warm water
1 ¹/₂ tablespoons active dry yeast
1 ¹/₈ teaspoons granulated sugar
2 ¹/₂ cups warm water
1 ¹/₈ cups nonfat dry milk powder
³/₄ cup (1 ¹/₂ sticks) butter, melted
1 ¹/₈ teaspoons salt
3 cups flour (combination of white, whole wheat, rye, oat, buckwheat, yellow
  cornmeal, or blue cornmeal)
3 eggs
¹/₂ teaspoon baking soda
Pure maple syrup, warmed

Put the ³/₄ cup water into a large bowl and sprinkle in the yeast and sugar. Let dissolve for 5 minutes.

Add the 2 ¹/₂ cups water, the milk, butter, salt, and flours to the yeast mixture and whisk until smooth and blended. Cover the bowl with plastic wrap and let stand overnight at room temperature. (The batter will rise to double its original volume.)

Before baking the waffles, beat in the eggs, then add the baking soda and stir until well combined. (The batter will be thin.) Pour ¹/₂ to ³/₄ cup batter into a very hot waffle iron and bake until golden and crisp. Serve immediately with the warm syrup.

Variation: Top with fresh strawberries and whipped cream or sliced bananas, toasted coconut, and sliced roasted almonds. Dust with confectioners' sugar.

YIELD: 8 SERVINGS

THE SPENCER HOUSE
SAN FRANCISCO, CALIFORNIA

Hearthstone Inn French Toast

6 eggs, beaten
¹/₂ cup packaged baking mix
2 tablespoons granulated sugar
1 ¹/₂ cups milk
¹/₂ teaspoon ground cinnamon
¹/₂ teaspoon ground nutmeg
1 loaf French bread, cut into 1-inch
  slices
Vegetable oil
1 recipe Spiced Butter
  (*see recipe below*)
1 recipe Gingered Whipped Cream
  (*see recipe below*)

In a large bowl, blend together the eggs, baking mix, sugar, milk, cinnamon, and nutmeg until smooth. Dip the bread slices in the batter until covered but not soaked.

In a large skillet, heat 1 inch of the oil. Add the bread slices and cook until golden brown on both sides. Serve immediately with the *Spiced Butter* and *Gingered Whipped Cream.*

YIELD: 4 TO 6 SERVINGS

Hearthstone Inn

Dot, Ruth, and Mark are all quick to point out that the *Hearthstone Inn French Toast* has become a breakfast tradition at their twenty-room Victorian inn at the foot of Pikes Peak. When we filmed their episode over the holidays, the inn was full of repeat guests who make it a seasonal tradition to bring a new handmade ornament for the inn's Christmas trees. No wonder they have three trees!

Spiced Butter

¹/₂ cup softened butter or margarine
3 tablespoons firmly packed brown
  sugar
¹/₄ teaspoon ground cinnamon
¹/₄ teaspoon ground allspice
¹/₈ teaspoon ground nutmeg

In a small bowl, combine all of the ingredients and beat until fluffy. Makes about ³/₄ cup.

Gingered Whipped Cream

One 8-ounce container whipping cream
5 to 6 pieces crystallized ginger, finely diced

In a medium-sized bowl, whip the cream until stiff but not buttery. Fold in the ginger. Cover and chill for at least 6 hours. Makes 1 cup.

HEARTHSTONE INN
COLORADO SPRINGS, COLORADO

Mast Farm Inn Stuffed French Toast

2 loaves dense French bread
One 8-ounce package cream cheese, at
  room temperature
One 15-ounce carton ricotta cheese
Peach or apricot preserves
2 cups milk
12 eggs
2 tablespoons pure vanilla extract
1/2 teaspoon salt
Generous sprinkling ground nutmeg
Vegetable oil

Mast Farm Inn

Two of the nicest people in the inn-keeping business, Sibyl and Francis Pressly, have breathed life into this historic farm and have made it possible for you to overnight in a very nicely appointed and fully converted blacksmith shop. "Inn Country USA" viewers have let us know that Sibyl's *Stuffed French Toast* is worth every calorie!

Cut the bread diagonally into 1/2 to 3/4-inch slices. (Do not cut off the crust.) In a medium-sized bowl, blend together both cheeses with a fork until smooth. Spread the cheese mixture on one side of each slice of bread, but do not spread to the edges. Top cheese side of one slice of bread with 1 teaspoon preserves and press the second slice of bread on top, cheese sides together. Cover with plastic wrap and refrigerate for several hours or overnight.

Place the chilled bread slices in a single layer in a shallow baking pan. In a blender, blend together the milk, eggs, vanilla, salt, and nutmeg for 5 seconds on medium speed. Pour the milk mixture over the bread slices. Let the bread soak for 5 to 10 minutes, then turn to coat both sides.

In a large skillet, heat 1/4-inch of the oil and sauté the bread slices on both sides until golden brown (3 slices per serving). Serve immediately with raspberry jam or other fruit syrup.

YIELD: 6 TO 8 SERVINGS

MAST FARM INN
VALLE CRUCIS, NORTH CAROLINA

Stuffed French Toast

³/₄ cup softened cream cheese
²/₃ cup orange marmalade
2 tablespoons honey
5 eggs
1 cup fresh orange juice
12 slices slightly frozen bread
Confectioners' sugar
Orange slices

In a small bowl, combine the cream cheese, marmalade, and honey and gently stir until just combined. In a medium-sized, shallow bowl, whisk together the eggs and orange juice.

Spread on each slice of bread the cream cheese mixture and top with another slice of bread. Dip the "sandwiches" in the egg mixture and place in a large, lightly buttered frying pan. Cook until browned on both sides. Cut into triangles and sprinkle with the sugar. Serve immediately with the orange slices.

YIELD: 6 SERVINGS

THE MAGNOLIA PLANTATION BED & BREAKFAST INN
GAINESVILLE, FLORIDA

Roberta's Baked French Toast

1 baguette, sliced diagonally 1 inch
  thick
5 eggs
1 cup half-and-half
1 cup milk
³/₄ teaspoon ground nutmeg
³/₄ teaspoon ground cinnamon
¹/₂ tablespoon pure vanilla extract

Topping:
¹/₄ cup (¹/₂ stick) butter, melted
¹/₂ cup packed light brown sugar
1 tablespoon light corn syrup
¹/₂ cup chopped pecans

The Gastonian

Hugh and Roberta Lineberger act as if
they have been innkeepers all of their
lives. These transplanted Californians
have become such a hit in the historic
community of Savannah, Georgia,
they have become "family." *Roberta's
Baked French Toast* and egg dishes are
part of the reason that this inn has become the only Four-Star and Four-
Diamond Inn in the entire state of
Georgia.

Butter an 8-inch square baking pan and layer the bread in two layers. In a blender
or food processor, mix together the remaining ingredients and slowly pour the mixture over the bread. Cover and refrigerate overnight.

Preheat oven to 350° F. To make the topping: In a medium-sized bowl, mix together in order all of the ingredients. Spread the topping over the chilled bread slices
and bake, uncovered, for 1 hour.

YIELD: 6 SERVINGS

*The Gastonian
Savannah, Georgia*

Southwestern Omelettes

2 cups cooked ground ham
$1/2$ cup sliced green onions
$1/2$ cup chopped green bell peppers
$2 1/2$ cups shredded cheddar cheese
Eight 5-inch flour tortillas
4 eggs, beaten
2 cups light cream or milk
1 tablespoon all-purpose flour
Salt to taste
$1/4$ teaspoon garlic powder
Dash Tabasco sauce

Grease a 12 x 17-inch baking pan. In a medium-sized bowl, combine the ham, onions, and bell peppers. Place $1/3$ cup of the mixture and 3 tablespoons of the cheese on the edge of each tortilla and roll up. Arrange the tortillas seam side down in the prepared pan.

In a separate bowl, mix together the eggs, cream, flour, salt, garlic powder, and Tabasco sauce and pour the mixture over the tortillas. Cover and refrigerate for several hours or overnight.

Preheat oven to 350° F. Bake the tortillas, uncovered, for 45 to 50 minutes. Sprinkle with the remaining cheese and bake for 3 minutes more, or until the cheese is melted. Let stand for 10 minutes before serving. Serve.

YIELD: 8 SERVINGS

THE GASTONIAN
SAVANNAH, GEORGIA

Spinach, Mushroom & Ham Omelette in Lemon-Dill Sauce

1 recipe Lemon-Dill Sauce
   (*see recipe below*)
2 tablespoons olive oil
8 large fresh mushrooms, washed and
   coarsely chopped
Seasoned salt to taste
Crushed dried red peppers
Sherry
6 eggs
4 egg whites
Dash salt
1 tablespoon vegetable oil
4 ounces Virginia baked ham, cut
   into julienned strips
1 bunch fresh spinach, trimmed,
   steamed, and well drained
Fresh parsley, chopped
Thin strips red bell pepper
Thin strips yellow bell pepper

The Oaks Bed & Breakfast Inn

Margaret and Tom Ray literally taught Christiansburg, Virginia, what a century-old Queen Anne Victorian with 300-year-old oak trees could become in the hands of dedicated innkeepers. Margaret is a multitalented hostess and chef who has made it her business to keep track of what guests at The Oaks prefer most. Her *Spinach, Mushroom & Ham Omelette* springs to life with the creative addition of a *Lemon-Dill Sauce* and is a favorite with her guests.

In a medium-sized skillet, heat the olive oil and sauté the mushrooms. Add the seasoned salt and a sprinkle of the red peppers. Sauté for about 1 minute more, then add a splash of the sherry. Remove from heat and set aside.

Heat a 14-inch, covered omelette pan on medium heat. In a medium-sized bowl, beat together the 6 eggs, 4 egg whites, and dash salt. Add the vegetable oil to the hot omelette pan, then add the beaten egg mixture. Lift the edges and let the uncooked eggs run under. Cover and repeat until the egg mixture is nearly cooked. Add the reserved mushrooms, the ham, and spinach to one half of the omelette. Flip the other half of the omelette over the vegetables and cover until the center is heated through.

Remove from heat and cut into fourths. Place one fourth on each serving plate and spoon the *Lemon-Dill Sauce* over each serving. Garnish with the parsley and strips of the bell peppers. Serve immediately.

YIELD: 4 SERVINGS

Lemon-Dill Sauce

1/4 cup (1/2 stick) butter
1/4 cup all-purpose flour
2 tablespoons chopped fresh chives, or
  2 teaspoons dried chives
2 tablespoons chopped fresh dill, or
  2 teaspoons dried dill
1 teaspoon crushed dried red peppers

1 teaspoon salt
4 cups skim milk
2 to 3 tablespoons fresh lemon juice
4 egg yolks

In the top of a double boiler, melt the butter over simmering water. Stir in the flour, herbs, red peppers, and salt. Whisk in the milk and continue to whisk until the sauce begins to thicken. In a small bowl, combine the lemon juice and egg yolks and slightly beat together. Add the lemon juice mixture to the sauce, stirring constantly. Continue to cook, stirring occasionally, for about 15 minutes. Add more milk, if needed, to make the sauce a thin consistency. Keep warm in a water bath.

THE OAKS BED & BREAKFAST INN
CHRISTIANSBURG, VIRGINIA

Eggs Florentine with Creamy Cheese Sauce

8 eggs, slightly beaten
One 8-ounce carton cottage cheese
8 ounces Swiss cheese, grated
8 ounces feta cheese, cubed
$^1/_4$ cup ($^1/_2$ stick) softened butter
Two 10-ounce packages frozen
   chopped spinach, thawed and
   drained
1 teaspoon ground nutmeg
1 recipe Creamy Cheese Sauce
   (see recipe below)

Preheat oven to 350° F. In a large bowl, combine the eggs, all of the cheeses, and the butter and mix well. Stir in the spinach and nutmeg.

Divide the mixture into greased 8-inch ramekins and bake for 30 to 45 minutes, or until a tester inserted in the center comes out clean. Ladle 1 $^1/_2$ tablespoons of the *Creamy Cheese Sauce* over each ramekin and serve.

YIELD: 8 SERVINGS

Creamy Cheese Sauce

2 tablespoons butter
3 tablespoons all-purpose flour
2 cups milk
2 cups grated Monterey Jack cheese
$^1/_2$ teaspoon salt
$^1/_4$ teaspoon ground mustard
$^1/_4$ teaspoon cayenne pepper

In a medium-sized saucepan, melt the butter. Stir in the flour and cook, stirring constantly, for 3 to 5 minutes. Add the milk and cook, stirring constantly, until the sauce begins to thicken and bubble. Stir in the cheese and seasonings and cook until the cheese is melted. Makes 2 to 3 cups.

The Gingerbread Mansion
Ferndale, California

Egg Blossoms with Hollandaise

6 sheets phyllo pastry, thawed
6 tablespoons (³/₄ stick) butter, melted
¹/₄ cup grated Parmesan cheese
3 cups torn fresh spinach
12 eggs
Salt and freshly ground black pepper
  to taste
¹/₄ cup finely chopped green onions
1 recipe Hollandaise Sauce
  (see recipe below)
Ground paprika

Lightly brush one sheet of the pastry with the butter. Layer a second sheet on top and brush with the butter. Cut these sheets into 6 equal squares. Repeat the procedure with the remaining pastry. (Cover the pastry with a slightly damp tea towel when not using to prevent drying and cracking.) Stack the 3 squares together, fanning in a spiral. Grease a 12-cup muffin pan and press the stacked squares into each cup to form a basket.

Preheat oven to 350° F. Sprinkle the bottoms of the cups with the cheese and spinach, reserving some cheese and spinach for the serving plate. Break 1 egg into each cup and season with the salt and black pepper. Sprinkle the tops with the onions and bake for 20 minutes, or until golden brown and the eggs are set.

Shred the remaining spinach and arrange in a crisscross pattern on each serving plate. Center 2 blossoms in the spinach bed and top with 1 ¹/₂ tablespoons of the *Hollandaise Sauce*. Sprinkle with the paprika and serve immediately.

YIELD: 6 SERVINGS

Hollandaise Sauce

4 egg yolks
3 tablespoons fresh lemon juice
¹/₂ cup (1 stick) butter

In a small saucepan, whisk together the egg yolks and lemon juice on very low heat. Add ¹/₄ cup of the butter and stir constantly until melted.

Add the remaining butter, stirring constantly, until the butter is melted and the sauce thickens. Makes 2 cups.

THE LOVELANDER BED & BREAKFAST INN
LOVELAND, COLORADO

Decadent Bread

1 loaf French bread, cut into
  1 1/2-inch-thick slices
2 eggs
3/4 cup granulated sugar
1 cup half-and-half
1/2 cup (1 stick) butter, melted
1 tablespoon pure vanilla extract
1 teaspoon ground nutmeg
1 teaspoon ground cinnamon
Fresh blueberries, rinsed

Herlong Mansion

Besides being the setting for a Holly-wood movie, Micanopy, Florida, is also the location of the Herlong Mansion. Sonny Howard is one of the most gifted innkeepers that we have encountered in the production of "Inn Country USA." His *Decadent Bread* will no doubt become one of those lazy weekend morning breakfast staples in your own home.

Preheat oven to 350° F. Place 1 slice of the bread into each of 6 small ramekins. In a medium-sized bowl, mix together the remaining ingredients, except the blueberries, and pour half of this mixture among the ramekins. Let stand for 5 to 10 minutes.

Turn the bread over and divide the remaining egg mixture among the ramekins. Bake for 40 to 50 minutes. Garnish with the blueberries and serve immediately.

YIELD: 6 SERVINGS

HERLONG MANSION
MICANOPY, FLORIDA

1842 Inn Savory Egg Casserole

¹/2 cup croutons
8 slices bacon
¹/4 cup chopped onions
4 eggs, beaten
2 cups milk
¹/2 teaspoon ground mustard
Salt to taste
Dash freshly ground black pepper
1 cup shredded cheddar cheese

In a 2-quart baking dish, place the croutons and set aside. In a small skillet, cook the bacon. Drain the bacon on paper towels and crumble. In the bacon fat, sauté the onions for 3 to 5 minutes or until tender. Drain off fat. In a medium-sized bowl, stir together the eggs, milk, mustard, salt, and black pepper until well combined.

Preheat oven to 350° F. Sprinkle the cheese over the reserved croutons and pour in the egg mixture. Sprinkle the crumbled bacon on top and bake for 50 to 60 minutes, or until the eggs puff. Remove and let stand for 5 minutes. Serve.

YIELD: 6 SERVINGS

1842 INN
MACON, GEORGIA

Featherbed Eggs

Bread slices (any type)
14 eggs
1 1/2 cups milk
1 1/2 cups half-and-half
Choice of 1 cup: chopped ham, cooked,
*   drained bacon or sausage, shredded*
*   cheese, sliced fresh mushrooms, or*
*   any combination*
Choice of seasonings: chopped fresh
*   herbs, salt, freshly ground black or*
*   white pepper, ground spices*

Sea Crest by the Sea

Here's an 1885 Queen Anne Victorian in northern New Jersey that has been lovingly restored to a cherished seaside destination by John and Carol Kirby. Here are a two former fast laners who now spend more time on their antique bicycles and croquet than they do on the *Wall Street Journal*. The perfect refuge indeed.

Butter a 9 x 11-inch baking pan and fill with the bread slices. In a large bowl, beat the eggs until frothy. Add the milk and half-and-half and beat until light yellow. Pour the mixture over the bread and add choice of ingredients and seasonings. Cover and refrigerate for 6 to 8 hours or overnight.

Bake in a cold oven at 350° F for 1 hour 30 minutes or until lightly browned and puffy. Remove and let stand for 5 minutes. Serve.

YIELD: 6 TO 8 SERVINGS

SEA CREST BY THE SEA
SPRING LAKE, NEW JERSEY

Chili-Cheese Puff

10 eggs, beaten
$1/2$ cup all-purpose flour
1 teaspoon baking powder
One 16-ounce carton cottage cheese
1 cup shredded Monterey Jack cheese
1 cup shredded cheddar cheese
$1/2$ cup (1 stick) melted butter
One $7 1/2$-ounce can diced green chilies, drained

Preheat oven to 350° F. In a large bowl, combine all of the ingredients, except the chilies, and mix together well. Stir in the chilies.

Pour the mixture into a well-sprayed 9 x 13-inch baking pan and bake for 35 to 40 minutes, or until the top is lightly browned and the center is firm. Remove and let stand for 5 minutes. Serve.

YIELD: 8 SERVINGS

CHANNEL ROAD INN
SANTA MONICA, CALIFORNIA

Ricotta Torte with Red Pepper Sauce

Filling:
1 bunch fresh spinach, washed,
*   trimmed, and steamed*
1 cup ricotta cheese
¹/₄ cup grated Parmesan cheese
2 tablespoons finely chopped onions
1 egg
Pinch ground nutmeg
Salt and freshly ground black pepper
*   to taste*
1 recipe Red Pepper Sauce
*   (see recipe below)*

Crêpes:
1 cup milk
2 tablespoons melted butter
3 eggs
³/₄ cup unbleached all-purpose flour
3 tablespoons cornmeal
Pinch salt
1 tablespoon butter
Sour cream
Fresh basil or oregano leaves

To make the filling: In a food processor, blend together the steamed spinach, both cheeses, the onions, and egg. Set aside.

To make the crêpes: In a blender or food processor, blend together the first six ingredients and let the mixture

Turtleback Farm Inn

We have found a place on Puget Sound that will move you to reflect on everything from life to love to leeks. Orcas Island is arguably the most pleasant of all the islands in the San Juans, off the coast of Washington State. Here is a genuine Turtleback treat, *Ricotta Torte with Red Pepper Sauce*, a runaway hit with even your most discerning guest. Enjoy!

stand for at least 1 hour.

Lightly coat a 10-inch nonstick skillet with the 1 tablespoon butter. While tilting the skillet, add 2 tablespoons batter to thinly coat the bottom and cook the crêpe until the bubbles pop. Turn the crêpe and brown the other side. Place the finished crêpe on a large square of aluminum foil and spread one-fifth of the filling on the crêpe.

Preheat oven to 350° F. Prepare the second crêpe, stack on first crêpe, and again spread the filling. Repeat this procedure until five crêpes have been filled, with a sixth crêpe as a topping.

Seal the torte in the foil and heat in the oven for 15 minutes or until completely heated through.

Cut the torte into six wedges and place on small serving plates. Spoon the *Red Pepper Sauce* over each wedge and garnish with a dollop of the sour cream and the basil. Serve immediately.

YIELD: 6 SERVINGS

Red Pepper Sauce

3 medium red bell peppers
2 tablespoons butter
2 tablespoons olive oil
3 large cloves garlic, finely chopped
2 tablespoons finely chopped onions
¼ cup sliced fresh mushrooms
1 cup chicken stock
2 tablespoons heavy cream
Pinch dried basil
Salt and freshly ground black pepper to taste

Preheat oven to 425° F. Roast the bell peppers whole in the oven for 15 minutes, or until the skins begin to blacken. Remove and put into a plastic bag for about 10 minutes. Remove the bell peppers from the bag and let cool, then peel and seed.

In a small skillet, melt the butter with the oil and sauté the garlic, onions, and mushrooms for 3 to 5 minutes, or until the onions are translucent. In a food processor, combine the prepared bell peppers, sautéed garlic mixture, and stock and process until smooth.

Transfer to a small saucepan and simmer for about 5 minutes. Stir in the cream, basil, salt, and black pepper. Keep warm. Makes about 2 cups.

TURTLEBACK FARM INN
ORCAS ISLAND, WASHINGTON

Mexican Eggs

8 eggs, beaten
1 cup cottage cheese
1 cup heavy cream
Salt to taste
Tabasco sauce to taste
One 4-ounce can chopped green chilies
3 ounces grated cheddar cheese

Preheat oven to 350°F. In a large bowl, whisk together the eggs, cottage cheese, cream, salt, and Tabasco sauce. Stir in the chilies and cheese and mix together well.

Pour the mixture into a greased 10-inch quiche pan and bake for 35 to 40 minutes. Remove and let stand for 5 minutes. Serve.

YIELD: 6 SERVINGS

The White Swan/ Petite Auberge

In the middle of everything on San Francisco's Bush Street is a little country inn that might just as easily be located in a London suburb. The deep green hues and jewel tones of this English hunt country inn with their fireplaces, ignited by a flip of the switch, contrast beautifully with their country French-styled "sister" inn, Petite Auberge, a few steps farther up the street.

THE WHITE SWAN/PETITE AUBERGE
SAN FRANCISCO, CALIFORNIA

Salmon Cakes with Poached Eggs & Creamy Dill Sauce

7 tablespoons cornmeal
3 tablespoons all-purpose flour
$^1/_4$ teaspoon baking soda
Pinch salt
$^1/_2$ cup buttermilk
$^1/_2$ cup softened cream cheese
1 egg, lightly beaten
$^1/_2$ cup corn kernels
6 tablespoons finely chopped chives
12 finely chopped peperoncinis
4 ounces smoked salmon, chopped
2 to 3 tablespoons butter
6 eggs, poached
1 recipe Creamy Dill Sauce
  (see recipe below)

In a medium-sized bowl, mix together the first four ingredients. Stir in the buttermilk, cream cheese, and egg. Gently fold in the corn, chives, peperoncinis, and salmon and form the mixture into 3-inch cakes.

In a large skillet, melt the butter and fry the cakes on medium heat until golden brown. Top each serving with 1 poached egg and cover with the *Creamy Dill Sauce*. Serve immediately.

YIELD: 6 SERVINGS

The Mansakenning Carriage House

The idea of sitting down at the dining room table in a home built in 1853 and listed in the National Register of Historic Places makes whatever delicious breakfast that is being served that much more memorable. Michelle Dremann and her husband John have created an idyllic country inn in New York's historic Hudson River Valley. The *Salmon Cakes with Poached Eggs & Creamy Dill Sauce* is a true signature dish!

Creamy Dill Sauce

2 cups heavy cream
3 tablespoons chopped fresh dill

In a small saucepan, combine the cream and dill. Reduce by half. Serve.

*THE MANSAKENNING CARRIAGE HOUSE
RHINEBECK, NEW YORK*

Vegetable Tulip Cups

Crêpes:
1 cup cold milk
1 cup cold water
2 cups sifted all-purpose flour
4 eggs
4 tablespoons melted butter

Filling:
One 15-ounce carton ricotta cheese
3 tablespoons chopped onions
3 tablespoons chopped red bell peppers
2 eggs, beaten
½ teaspoon dried basil
¼ cup grated Parmesan cheese
2 cups grated zucchini
¼ cup heavy cream
Ground paprika
Fresh romaine lettuce leaves
1 large red bell pepper, sliced into
  rings

The Whitehall Inn

At this inn, cooking is a family affair. When we visited The Whitehall with our camera crew, we were pleasantly surprised that the children were just as enthusiastic about the process of creating in the kitchen as Mike and Suella. The original late 1700s deed for this home described it as a plantation. Although few vestiges of life two centuries ago remain today at Whitehall, the dedication to plantation-style entertaining certainly remains pleasantly in tact.

To make the crêpes: In a food processor, blend together all of the ingredients. Heat a crêpe pan and spray with oil. Ladle 2 tablespoons batter into the pan and swirl around to form a thin layer. Cook for 1 to 2 minutes, then turn and cook for 30 seconds on the other side. Repeat the procedure to make the remaining crêpes. As each crêpe is prepared, stack and set aside.

Preheat oven to 350° F. To make the filling: In a large bowl, combine the ricotta cheese, onions, bell peppers, and eggs and stir together well. Add the basil, Parmesan cheese, and zucchini and stir until well combined. Mix in the cream.

Spray a 12-cup muffin pan with oil. Spoon 1 to 2 tablespoons filling into the center of each crêpe and sprinkle with the paprika. Place each crêpe in a muffin cup and cover the pan with aluminum foil. Cut steam holes and bake for 25 minutes. Serve 2 to 3 crêpes per serving on a bed of the lettuce leaves.

Garnish with the bell pepper rings and serve immediately.

YIELD: 4 TO 6 SERVINGS

THE WHITEHALL INN
NEW HOPE, PENNSYLVANIA

Jalapeño Grit Cakes with Shrimp & Tasso Sauce

1 tablespoon butter
24 medium shrimp (26 to 35 count), peeled and deveined with tails
1 cup diced tasso ham
¹/₂ cup heavy cream
¹/₂ cup grated Parmesan cheese
1 cup cooked hot grits
3 jalapeño peppers, finely diced
Fresh chives, chopped

In a large skillet, melt the butter and sauté the shrimp and tasso ham on medium heat for 1 minute, or until the shrimp turns pink. Stir in the cream and cheese. Reduce heat to simmer and cook, stirring constantly, until the sauce thickens. Set aside and keep warm.

In a small bowl, mix together the hot grits and peppers and form the mixture into 4 cakes. Place 1 cake on each serving plate and pour the reserved sauce over the cakes. Garnish with the chives and serve immediately.

YIELD: 4 SERVINGS

BEAUFORT INN
BEAUFORT, SOUTH CAROLINA

Grits & Garlic Custard

$^3/_4$ *cup uncooked grits*
$2^1/_4$ *cups milk*
$^3/_4$ *cup heavy cream*
$^1/_2$ *tablespoon finely chopped garlic*
$^1/_2$ *teaspoon cracked black pepper*
$^3/_4$ *teaspoon kosher salt*
$^2/_3$ *cup grated smoked Gouda cheese*

Custard:
3 cups heavy cream
8 eggs, beaten
$^1/_2$ *tablespoon salt*
Pinch ground nutmeg
1 tablespoon pommery mustard

Inn at Blackberry Farm

The gently rolling Tennessee hills, south of Knoxville, provide a splendid platform for this inn where you leave your cares at home. Once you are registered at the Inn, everything is included—fly-fishing, golf carts, picnics, breakfasts, and dinners. If you are from the South, here is a recipe from chef John Fleer that will change the way you enjoy your grits. If you are among the uninitiated, try this terrific recipe to begin your relationship with this southern staple.

Grease ten 6-ounce ramekins. In a medium-sized saucepan, combine the grits, milk, cream, garlic, black pepper, and salt and simmer until the grits are fully cooked. Set aside and let cool.

Preheat oven to 300° F. To make the custard: In a large bowl, stir together all of the ingredients until well combined.

Place 2 tablespoons of the reserved grits mixture in each ramekin and top with 1 tablespoon of the cheese. Divide the custard mixture among the ramekins and bake for 30 minutes or until fully set.

Remove the ramekins and let cool in a water bath. Remove the set custard from the ramekins and place on small serving plates. Serve.

YIELD: 10 SERVINGS

INN AT BLACKBERRY FARM
WALLAND, TENNESSEE

Artichoke Heart Strudel

Two 14-ounce cans artichoke hearts (10 whole artichokes), chopped
1/2 cup mayonnaise
1/2 teaspoon garlic salt
1 egg
1 teaspoon Tabasco sauce
3/4 cup grated Parmesan cheese
One 8-ounce package phyllo pastry
1 cup (2 sticks) butter, melted
Dried bread crumbs

In a medium-sized bowl, mix together the first six ingredients until well blended. Chill until ready to use.

Place 1 sheet of the pastry on a work surface and brush on the butter to cover one half of the pastry. Sprinkle some bread crumbs over the buttered half. Fold the unbuttered half over the buttered half and repeat the procedure.

Working with the shorter side towards you, place 1 heaping tablespoon of the chilled filling in the center at the end and roll away from you (two rolls). Then fold in both sides of the pastry towards the center. (This will keep the filling from running out.) Continue rolling until you get to the end, always placing the end of the pastry on the bottom.

Preheat oven to 350° F. Brush the pastry with more butter and place on a baking sheet. Bake for 15 minutes or until golden brown. Let cool slightly. Cut and serve.

YIELD: 8 TO 10 SERVINGS

ROSE INN
ITHACA, NEW YORK

Spicy Buttermilk Coffee Cake

2 1/4 cups all-purpose flour
1/2 teaspoon salt
2 teaspoons ground cinnamon
1/4 teaspoon ground ginger
1 cup packed brown sugar
3/4 cup granulated sugar
3/4 cup corn oil
2 cups chopped pecans
1 teaspoon baking soda
1 teaspoon baking powder
1 egg, beaten
1 cup buttermilk

Victorian Inn on the Park

While producing "Inn Country USA," we have encountered inns that specialize in many different things. This historic landmark inn is just a hop, skip, and jump from Golden Gate Park, and one of the few that we have visited that specializes in baked goods. You will know that you have found the right place when you open the front door and smell the aromas from the oven!

Preheat oven to 350° F. In a large bowl, mix together the flour, salt, 1 teaspoon of the cinnamon, the ginger, both sugars, and the oil. In a medium-sized bowl, combine 3/4 cup of the flour mixture, the pecans, and remaining cinnamon and mix together well. Set aside.

Add the baking soda, baking powder, egg, and buttermilk to the sugar mixture and stir together well. Pour the batter into a greased 9 x 13-inch baking pan. Sprinkle the pecan mixture over the top and bake for 40 minutes. Let cool on a wire rack or serve warm.

YIELD: 8 SERVINGS

VICTORIAN INN ON THE PARK
SAN FRANCISCO, CALIFORNIA

CHAPTER 2

Appetizers

Sautéed Tiger Prawns with Garlic & Lemon

6 tablespoons (³/₄ stick) unsalted butter
16 large fresh black tiger or blacktail prawns (10 to 15 count),
  peeled and deveined
2 tablespoons finely chopped shallots
2 tablespoons finely chopped garlic
¹/₂ cup dry white wine or sherry
Juice of 1 lemon
2 tablespoons chopped fresh chervil
Salt and freshly ground black pepper to taste

In a large sauté pan, melt 2 tablespoons of the butter and sauté the prawns on medium-high heat for 2 minutes, or until the prawns turn pink. Add the shallots, garlic, and wine and cook for 4 minutes, or until the wine is reduced by about half.

Add the remaining butter, the lemon juice, and chervil. When the butter is completely melted, add the salt and black pepper. Serve immediately.

YIELD: 4 APPETIZER SERVINGS

CARTER HOUSE/HOTEL CARTER
EUREKA, CALIFORNIA

Bourbon Shrimp

2 tablespoons butter
10 large fresh shrimp (15 to 21 count), peeled and deveined with tails
2 tablespoons warm bourbon whiskey
½ to ¾ cup whipping cream
Salt and freshly ground black pepper to taste
Toasted bread, cut into triangles

In a large sauté pan, melt the butter and sauté the shrimp on medium-high heat for 2 minutes, or until the shrimp turn pink. Add the whiskey and flambé.

Add the cream and reduce until just slightly thick. Add the salt and black pepper. Serve immediately with the toast points.

YIELD: 4 APPETIZER SERVINGS

The Inn at Gristmill Square

The Inn at Gristmill Square is both charming and delightful and comes by its name quite honestly. There has been a mill on the present site on Warm Spring Run in the heart of Warm Springs, Virginia, continuously since 1771. The inn is a very attractive medley of five nineteenth-century buildings that have been remodeled to accommodate inn guests.

THE INN AT GRISTMILL SQUARE
WARM SPRINGS, VIRGINIA

Sweet Corn Pancakes with Gulf Shrimp

Pancakes:
2 small potatoes, peeled
$1/2$ teaspoon chopped fresh thyme
$1/2$ cup fresh corn kernels
Salt and freshly ground black pepper
  to taste
$1/2$ cup heavy cream
1 large egg, beaten

Sauce:
$1/4$ cup ($1/2$ stick) butter
2 shallots, chopped
1 clove garlic, chopped
$1/2$ cup dry vermouth
2 cups heavy cream
$1/2$ cup (1 stick) chilled butter

Noodles:
4 cups peanut oil
2 ounces uncooked bean thread noodles
2 tablespoons cajun spice

Shrimp:
2 tablespoons butter
Flour
12 large fresh shrimp (10 to 15
  count), peeled and deveined
  with tails
Salt and freshly ground black pepper
  to taste
$1/2$ cup washed drained fresh spinach
2 tablespoons finely chopped fresh
  thyme

To make the pancakes: In a small saucepan, cook the potatoes in water to cover for 20 minutes or until tender. Drain and let cool in a stainless steel bowl. When cool, mash the potatoes until smooth. Add the thyme, corn, salt, black pepper, cream, and egg and blend together well. Chill for 1 hour.

To make the sauce: In a medium-sized saucepan, melt the $1/4$ cup butter and sauté the shallots and garlic for 3 to 5 minutes or until tender. Deglaze the saucepan with the vermouth. Stir in the cream and reduce by half. Whisk in the $1/2$ cup butter until melted. In a blender or food processor, blend the mixture until smooth. Strain. Set aside and keep warm.

To make the noodles: In a large pot, heat the oil to 375° F. Quickly drop the noodles in the oil and cook for 2 to 3 seconds. Remove the noodles from the oil and drain on paper towels. Sprinkle with the cajun spice.

Preheat oven to 350° F. To make the shrimp: In a large sauté pan, melt the butter. Form 3 tablespoons of the chilled potato mixture into a patty and dredge in the flour. Repeat the procedure with the remaining potato mixture. Place the patties in the hot sauté pan and cook until brown on both sides. Place the pancakes on a rimmed baking sheet and finish cooking in the oven for 5 minutes.

Add the shrimp to the sauté pan, season with the salt and black pepper, and sauté until two-thirds done. Add the spinach and sauté until wilted.

Place the spinach in the center of each serving plate and center 1 pancake on top of the spinach. Arrange 3 shrimp around the pancake and place a small bundle of the noodles on top of the pancake. Drizzle the reserved sauce around the shrimp and over the noodles. Sprinkle with the thyme.

YIELD: 4 APPETIZER SERVINGS

JOSEPHINE'S BED & BREAKFAST
SEASIDE, FLORIDA

Smoked Shenandoah Trout Mousse with Dill Vin Blanc Sauce

1 teaspoon butter
2 shallots, chopped
12 ounces cream cheese, softened
8 ounces smoked Shenandoah trout,
  removed from bone
Juice of 1 lemon
1/4 cup white wine
1 tablespoon dried dill
Salt and freshly ground black pepper
  to taste
1 recipe Dill Vin Blanc Sauce
  (*see recipe below*)
Water crackers

In a small saucepan, melt the butter and sauté the shallots for 4 to 6 minutes or until browned. In a medium-sized bowl, combine the sautéed shallots, cream cheese, trout, lemon juice, wine, dill, salt, and black pepper and mix together with an electric mixer on low speed until well blended. Chill.

Serve the chilled trout mousse on the crackers with the *Dill Vin Blanc Sauce* on the side.

YIELD: 10 TO 12 APPETIZER
SERVINGS

Prospect Hill Plantation Inn

If you have not visited a country inn recently, you may be surprised at how sophisticated some of the inns have become under the thoughtful guidance of innkeepers who have merged their lifestyle into their profession. At Prospect Hill, the entire Sheehan family contributes to the inn regularly earning the 1732 Historic Plantation Four-Diamond Award and the enduring respect of inngoers from all over the world.

Dill Vin Blanc Sauce

1/2 tablespoon butter
2 tablespoons chopped onions
2 cups dry white wine
1 teaspoon fresh rosemary
1 teaspoon dried thyme
1/2 teaspoon freshly ground black
  pepper
Juice of 1/2 lemon
1 tablespoon clam juice
1/2 cup heavy cream

*¹/₂ tablespoon cornstarch mixed with
   dash cold water*
1 tablespoon dried dill

In a medium-sized saucepan, melt the butter and sauté the onions for 3 to 5 minutes or until translucent. Stir in the wine, rosemary, thyme, black pepper, lemon juice, and clam juice and bring to a medium boil. Reduce by one-third.

Strain the onions and herbs and discard. Return the liquid to the saucepan. Stir in the cream and bring to a slow boil, stirring constantly. Add the cornstarch mixture to thicken and continue to stir. Add the dill and cook for 1 minute more. Remove from heat and serve. Makes about 2 cups.

*PROSPECT HILL PLANTATION INN
TREVILIANS, VIRGINIA*

Crab Croquettes

1 pound fresh backfin crabmeat,
  picked and cleaned
2 tablespoons chopped fresh parsley
2 tablespoons grated onions
1 tablespoon fresh lemon juice
1 cup thick cream sauce
  (*choice of favorite*)
1 egg
1 teaspoon Worcestershire sauce
1/8 teaspoon freshly ground black
  pepper
2 drops Tabasco sauce (*optional*)
1 cup dried bread crumbs
1 teaspoon ground paprika
2 eggs, slightly beaten

The Chalfonte

The oldest, continuously operating hotel in Cape May, New Jersey, is the venerable Chalfonte. Built in 1876 by a northern hero of the War Between the States, Colonel Henry Sawyer, the hotel has developed a well-earned reputation for old-fashioned southern cooking and has even received accolades from the *Philadelphia Inquirer*, "The Chalfonte has spent more than 60 years preparing such southern-style delicacies as *Crab Croquettes* and *Spoon Bread*."

In a large bowl, combine the first nine ingredients and mix together with hands. Shape the mixture into croquettes. In a medium-sized bowl, stir together the bread crumbs, paprika, and eggs. Roll each croquette in the bread crumb mixture and let stand for 1 hour.

Fry the croquettes in deep fat at 375° F for 4 to 5 minutes or until browned. Serve immediately.

YIELD: 6 APPETIZER SERVINGS

THE CHALFONTE
CAPE MAY, NEW JERSEY

Smoked Salmon en Croûte

*4 ounces farmer's cheese or cream
 cheese*
1 pound cream cheese, softened
2 eggs, beaten
*8 ounces smoked salmon, cut into
 medium-sized chunks*
4 scallions, diced (green tops only)
1 tablespoon capers
¼ cup finely chopped fresh parsley
*Salt and freshly ground black pepper
 to taste*
18 sheets phyllo pastry
Melted butter
Poppy seeds

High Meadows

Whether you bike in or drive, you will be captivated by this cozy historic inn with a vineyard in the front yard. We have tried our share of salmon, but here is a recipe that adds just the touch to make you famous in your own kitchen.

In a medium-sized bowl, mix together the first eight ingredients and set aside.

Preheat oven to 375°F. Prepare 6 sheets of the pastry, following package directions. Place one third of the reserved salmon mixture on the pastry and roll as directed on package. Repeat the procedure two more times.

Brush the top of each roll with the melted butter and sprinkle with the poppy seeds. Make diagonal slashes across each top. Place the rolls on a jelly-roll pan and bake for 15 to 20 minutes. Let cool slightly. Cut into slices and serve immediately. Makes 3 rolls.

YIELD: VARIABLE APPETIZER SERVINGS

HIGH MEADOWS
SCOTTSVILLE, VIRGINIA

Quail & Radicchio

1 cup olive oil
4 quail, dressed
2 heads fresh radicchio lettuce
1 cup balsamic vinegar
4 cloves garlic, chopped
1 cup cubed cooked acorn squash
8 cloves blackened garlic

In a large sauté pan, heat the oil on high heat and sear the quail for 2 to 5 minutes on each side or until browned and thoroughly cooked. Remove and drain on paper towels. Keep warm. Add the radicchio to the hot oil and sauté for 1 to 2 minutes. Remove and place the radicchio on four serving plates.

Deglaze the pan with the vinegar and chopped garlic. Place the cooked squash on each plate and add the warm quail. Drizzle with the balsamic glaze and garnish with the blackened garlic. Serve immediately.

YIELD: 4 APPETIZER SERVINGS

GREYFIELD INN
CUMBERLAND ISLAND, GEORGIA

Pâté Maison

1 pound 8 ounces chicken livers
1 pound lean ground pork
8 ounces pork sausage
1 tablespoon finely chopped shallots
2 tablespoons chopped fresh parsley
1 teaspoon freshly ground black pepper
¹/₂ teaspoon ground ginger
¹/₂ teaspoon ground cinnamon
1 ¹/₂ teaspoons salt
2 tablespoons brandy
2 tablespoons white wine
Bacon strips
Thin rye bread rounds

In a food processor, combine all of the ingredients, except the bacon and bread, and process until well combined.

Preheat oven to 350° F. Line the bottom and sides of an 8-cup pâté mold with the bacon, overlapping slightly. Fill the mold with the mixture in stages, packing down after each addition. Cover the mold with heavy aluminum foil and bake in a water bath (about 1 inch around the mold) for 2 hours 30 minutes.

Cool in the mold with a weight on top of the pâté. Slice and serve with the bread rounds.

YIELD: 8 TO 10 APPETIZER SERVINGS

THE INN AT GRISTMILL SQUARE
WARM SPRINGS, VIRGINIA

Leek & Cheddar Tart with Roasted Red Pepper Sauce

3 tablespoons butter

2 1/2 cups washed chopped leeks

1 small onion, chopped

2 cloves garlic, chopped

1/4 teaspoon ground fennel

2 tablespoons all-purpose flour

1 cup milk

3 ounces cheddar cheese, grated

2 eggs, beaten

Salt and freshly ground black pepper
  to taste

Ground nutmeg to taste

One 10-inch prebaked tart shell

1 recipe Roasted Red Pepper Sauce
  (*see recipe below*)

The Darby Field Inn

When we filmed the Darby Field episode, we were all struck by the grandeur of the inn's giant stone hearth in front of a window framing the White Mountain National Forest. And the *Leek & Cheddar Tart with Roasted Red Pepper Sauce*— Marc and Maria Donaldson truly do understand the beauty of complementary taste and texture.

In a large sauté pan, melt the butter and sauté the leeks, onion, and garlic on medium heat for 4 to 5 minutes, or until the leeks are soft. Stir in the fennel and flour and cook, stirring constantly, for 2 minutes. Add the milk and cook, stirring constantly, for 4 to 5 minutes, or until the mixture is thickened.

Preheat oven to 350° F. Remove the mixture from the heat and stir in the cheese and eggs. Add the salt, black pepper, and nutmeg. Pour the mixture into the prebaked tart shell and bake for 25 minutes, or until the custard is set and the pastry is browned. Remove and let stand for 5 minutes. Cut into wedges and serve warm with the *Roasted Red Pepper Sauce.*

YIELD: 8 APPETIZER SERVINGS

Roasted Red Pepper Sauce

2 medium red bell peppers

1 tablespoon olive oil

1 small onion, chopped

1 tablespoon chopped garlic

1 cup white wine
1 cup vegetable or chicken stock
1 tablespoon tomato paste
Salt and freshly ground black pepper
* to taste*
Tabasco sauce to taste

Roast the bell peppers under the broiler until the skin is blistered and charred. Wrap the charred peppers in wet paper towels for 10 to 15 minutes to steam the skin. Remove the paper towels and peel off the skin under cold running water. Seed and devein the peppers and set aside.

In a medium-sized saucepan, heat the oil and sauté the onion and garlic for 3 to 5 minutes, or until the onion is translucent. Add the reserved peppers and the remaining ingredients and simmer for 20 to 30 minutes.

In a blender or food processor, puree the sauce and serve warm. Makes about 2 ¹/₂ cups.

THE DARBY FIELD INN
CONWAY, NEW HAMPSHIRE

Onion Tarts

Pastry for one 9-inch pie shell

Filling:
3 tablespoons butter
1 medium onion, chopped
1 clove garlic, finely chopped
¼ cup heavy cream
¼ cup grated Parmesan cheese
Dash cayenne pepper
Dash freshly ground black pepper
¼ teaspoon salt

1842 Inn

Phil Jenkins, the innkeeper of this Macon, Georgia, Greek Revival masterpiece likes to tickle the ivories for his guests during afternoon high tea. This inn is an elegantly serene montage of good taste in service, design, and food. Try the *Onion Tarts*. You are in for a very delicious surprise!

Press walnut-sized pieces of the pastry dough evenly into 24 miniature tart shells and set aside.

Preheat oven to 350° F. To make the filling: In a medium-sized skillet, melt the butter and sauté the onion and garlic for 3 to 5 minutes, or until the onion is translucent. Stir in the remaining ingredients and mix until well combined.

Fill the reserved tart shells to the top (the onions will settle during baking) and bake for 20 to 30 minutes, or until the crust is golden brown. Remove and let stand for 5 minutes. Serve warm. Makes 24 miniature tarts.

YIELD: 6 TO 8 APPETIZER SERVINGS

1842 INN
MACON, GEORGIA

Savory Ham & Cheese Tartlets

Crust:
2 cups all-purpose flour
Pinch salt
$^1/_2$ cup (1 stick) cold butter
1 egg yolk
1 teaspoon fresh lemon juice
2 tablespoons cold water

Filling:
$^3/_4$ cup grated sharp cheddar cheese
1 cup cooked cubed ham
1 egg
$^1/_2$ cup milk
Salt and freshly ground black pepper
  to taste
Fresh oregano, finely chopped
Fresh basil, finely chopped
Fresh parsley, chopped

To make the crust: In a medium-sized bowl, mix together the flour and salt. Cut in the butter with a pastry blender until the mixture resembles coarse meal. In a small bowl, stir together the egg yolk and lemon juice and add to the flour mixture. Add enough of the cold water to bind the dough together and give the consistency needed. Turn the dough out onto a floured surface and knead several times. Wrap in wax paper and chill for 30 minutes.

Preheat oven to 350° F. Grease a 12-cup, 2-inch tartlet pan. Roll out the chilled pastry on a lightly floured surface. Cut out 12 rounds with a 2$^1/_2$-inch cutter and line each cup of the prepared pan with 1 pastry round.

To make the filling: Sprinkle each round with 1 tablespoon of the cheese and sprinkle some ham into each cup. In a medium-sized bowl, whisk together the egg, milk, salt, and black pepper. Pour the egg mixture into the pastry shells and sprinkle with the herbs. Bake for 35 for 45 minutes, or until the filling is set. Remove and let stand for 5 minutes. Serve warm. Makes 12 tartlets.

YIELD: VARIABLE APPETIZER
SERVINGS

THE GINGERBREAD MANSION
FERNDALE, CALIFORNIA

Baked Mushrooms Stuffed with Country Sausage

1 pound bulk sausage
¹/₂ cup finely chopped fresh parsley
¹/₂ cup grated Parmesan cheese
¹/₂ cup finely chopped scallions
2 eggs, lightly beaten
¹/₄ cup (¹/₂ stick) butter
25 large fresh mushroom caps

In a large skillet, cook the sausage on medium heat until the sausage is broken into small pieces and is no longer pink. Drain on paper towels. In a medium-sized bowl, mix together the parsley, ¹/₄ cup of the cheese, the scallions, and eggs. Set aside.

Preheat oven to 400° F. In a large skillet, melt the butter and sauté the mushroom caps for 1 to 2 minutes, rolling the caps around in the skillet. Let cool.

Divide the reserved sausage mixture among the mushroom caps, mounding slightly. Place the caps in a lightly buttered baking pan. Sprinkle each cap with about ¹/₂ teaspoon of the remaining cheese and bake for 10 minutes. Serve immediately. Makes 25 mushrooms.

YIELD: VARIABLE APPETIZER SERVINGS

THE FEARRINGTON HOUSE
PITTSBORO, NORTH CAROLINA

Florentine Feta-Stuffed Mushrooms

2 tablespoons olive oil
¼ teaspoon chopped garlic
3 tablespoons chopped Spanish
* onions*
3 tablespoons chopped red bell
* peppers*
1 cup packed chopped fresh spinach
Salt and freshly ground black pepper
* to taste*
2 tablespoons cottage cheese
2 tablespoons crumbled feta cheese
½ cup fresh bread crumbs
12 large fresh mushroom caps
Splash white wine
1 tablespoon clarified butter
¼ cup chopped walnuts

Asa Ransom House

This inn holds the record for how long one reservation traveled to be processed. A Buffalo, New York, viewer happened to see an episode of "Inn Country USA" being relayed off a satellite from KRMA in Denver. The viewer called Denver to request more information about Asa Ransom and was surprised to learn that the inn was less than 30 miles away in Clarence, New York! The viewer consequently visited this charming inn and loved it.

Preheat oven to 400° F. In a medium-sized skillet, heat the oil and sauté the garlic, onions, and bell peppers for 3 to 5 minutes, or until the onions are translucent. Add the spinach and continue to sauté. Stir in the salt, black pepper, and both cheeses. Add the bread crumbs and mix well to combine.

Stuff each mushroom cap with the mixture and place the stuffed mushrooms in a baking pan. Splash with the wine and drizzle on the butter.

Top with the walnuts and bake for 8 to 10 minutes. Serve immediately. Makes 12 mushrooms.

YIELD: VARIABLE APPETIZER SERVINGS

ASA RANSOM HOUSE
CLARENCE, NEW YORK

Mushrooms Kathleen

16 large fresh mushroom caps
1 cup (2 sticks) softened butter or margarine
4 slices bacon, cooked, drained, and crumbled
2 tablespoons finely chopped shallots
1 tablespoon chopped fresh parsley
4 cloves garlic, finely chopped
2 tablespoons cognac brandy (optional)
16 fresh bay scallops
16 toast points

Preheat oven to 350° F. Place the mushroom caps hollow side up in a baking pan. In a medium-sized bowl, stir together the butter, bacon, shallots, parsley, garlic, and brandy.

Place 1 teaspoon of the butter mixture in each mushroom cap and top with 1 scallop. Cover each scallop-filled mushroom with 1 rounded teaspoon of the remaining butter mixture and bake for 20 to 25 minutes or until golden brown. Serve hot with the toast points. Makes 16 mushrooms.

YIELD: VARIABLE APPETIZER SERVINGS

Schumacher's New Prague Hotel
New Prague, Minnesota

Spinach Enchiladas

4 cups milk
1/2 cup (1 stick) butter
1/2 cup all-purpose flour
1 large fresh California green chili
  pepper, seeded and finely chopped
2 fresh jalapeño peppers, seeded and
  finely chopped
1 teaspoon salt

1/2 teaspoon white pepper
1 teaspoon garlic powder
2 tablespoons olive oil
1 medium onion, chopped
Three 10-ounce packages frozen
  spinach, cooked and drained
1 pound Swiss cheese, grated
Ten 8-inch flour tortillas

In a medium-sized saucepan, heat the milk until hot and set aside. In a large frying pan, melt the butter and stir in the flour to make a roux. Add the reserved hot milk and cook, stirring constantly, for 5 to 7 minutes or until creamy. (Thin with water if the sauce becomes too thick.) Add the chili pepper, jalapeño pepper, salt, white pepper, and garlic powder and stir until well blended. Set aside.

In a large saucepan, heat the oil and sauté the onion for 3 to 5 minutes or until translucent. Add the spinach and cook for 5 to 10 minutes. Stir 1 cup of the sauce into the spinach mixture and mix together well.

Preheat oven to 375° F. Reserve half of the cheese for the topping and divide the remaining cheese into 10 portions. Put 1 portion of the cheese on each tortilla, top with 1/2 cup of the spinach mixture, and sprinkle 2 1/2 teaspoons of the reserved cheese on top of the spinach. Roll each tortilla, tuck the ends underneath, and place the tortillas in a large baking pan.

Cover each tortilla with a ladle of sauce and sprinkle with the remaining reserved cheese. Bake for 15 to 20 minutes or until golden brown. Serve immediately.

YIELD: 10 APPETIZER SERVINGS

MAST FARM INN
VALLE CRUCIS, NORTH CAROLINA

Savory Sage Biscuits with Chili & Roasted Garlic Jam

8 cups sifted all-purpose flour
4 tablespoons baking powder
2 teaspoons granulated sugar
2 teaspoons ground cumin
2 teaspoons freshly ground black
 pepper
2 teaspoons dried sage
4 teaspoons granulated sugar
1 1/2 cups (3 sticks) cold sweet butter,
 cut into 1/4-inch cubes
3 cups cold milk
1 recipe Chili & Roasted Garlic Jam
 (*see recipe below*)

The Lovelander Bed & Breakfast Inn

Besides this great appetizer, this inn offers an egg dish that is one of the most often requested recipes in the "Inn Country USA" television series (see page 27). Bob and Marilyn Wiltgen have put enough of their hearts into The Lovelander to qualify them as official goodwill ambassadors of the little Colorado town that celebrates February 14th the way the rest of the nation celebrates July 4th!

In a large mixing bowl, mix together all of the dry ingredients until well combined. Cut the butter into the flour mixture with a pastry blender until the mixture is the consistency of small peas. Add the milk all at once and stir with a spatula until you have a loose ball. Turn the dough out onto a lightly floured surface and knead 10 to 12 times, just until the dough is gathered and blended together.

Preheat oven to 450° F. Press down the dough with hands. With a 2-inch biscuit cutter with fluted edge, cut the dough, pressing straight down. (Any twisting motion will cause the biscuits to be lopsided when baked.)

Place the biscuits on a large baking sheet lined with parchment paper and bake for 8 to 10 minutes. Serve hot with the *Chili & Roasted Garlic Jam*. Makes 3 dozen small biscuits.

YIELD: VARIABLE APPETIZER SERVINGS

Chili & Roasted Garlic Jam

2 cups peeled whole garlic cloves
12 to 14 fresh Anaheim chili
  peppers
2 tablespoons brown sugar

Preheat oven to 350°F. In a medium-sized baking pan, roast the garlic cloves for 30 minutes or until golden brown and soft. Set aside.

Roast the chili peppers under the broiler until the skin is charred. Place the peppers in a plastic bag and set aside for 10 to 15 minutes or until cool enough to handle. Peel away all the blackened skin and remove the stems and seeds. Cut the peppers into $1\frac{1}{2}$-inch squares and set aside.

In a large saucepan, combine the reserved garlic and peppers and the sugar and cook on medium heat, stirring frequently, until the brown sugar glazes over the garlic and peppers and the aromas are pronounced. Serve warm. Makes 4 cups.

THE LOVELANDER BED & BREAKFAST INN
LOVELAND, COLORADO

Open-Faced Tomato Sandwiches

4 slices firmly textured brown bread
¹/₂ cup mayonnaise
¹/₂ teaspoon curry powder or to taste
Butter, softened
3 Italian plum tomatoes, thinly sliced
Cream cheese, softened
Fresh parsley, finely chopped

Cut the bread into small rounds or daisy shapes with a cookie cutter, approximately 3 rounds per slice of bread. Wrap in plastic wrap and set aside.

In a small bowl, stir together the mayonnaise and curry powder. Spread a thin layer of the butter on each round, then spread with the mayonnaise mixture. Top with 1 tomato slice.

Place the cream cheese in a pastry bag and pipe a tiny rosette in the center of each tomato. Garnish with a pinch of the parsley and serve. Makes 12 canapés.

YIELD: VARIABLE APPETIZER SERVINGS

CASTLE MARNE
DENVER, COLORADO

Cucumber Sandwiches

4 slices thinly sliced white bread
1 small cucumber, peeled and finely chopped
¹/₄ cup softened cream cheese
3 tablespoons prepared horseradish
¹/₂ teaspoon onion salt
Butter, softened
Cream cheese, softened
Fresh herb leaves

Cut the bread into daisy or other shapes with a cookie cutter, approximately 3 shapes per slice of bread. Wrap in plastic wrap and set aside.

In a small bowl, mix together the cucumber, ¹/₄ cup cream cheese, horseradish, and onion salt. Spread a thin layer of the butter on each piece of bread, then spread with the cucumber mixture.

Place the cream cheese in a pastry bag and pipe a tiny rosette on top of each sandwich. Garnish with the herb leaves and serve. Makes 12 canapés.

YIELD: VARIABLE APPETIZER SERVINGS

CASTLE MARNE
DENVER, COLORADO

Skordalia

1 pound potatoes, peeled, chopped,
  and cooked
1/4 cup pureed roasted garlic
1/2 cup dried bread crumbs
1 tablespoon fresh lemon juice
Salt and freshly ground black
  pepper to taste
1/4 cup olive oil
1/4 cup chopped scallions
1/8 cup chopped pitted black olives
Flat bread, grilled

Rabbit Hill Inn

There are some inns that just seem to stir the romantic soul, and this showpiece in Lower Waterford, Vermont, is most certainly one of them. This Four-Diamond award-winning 1795 Federal Period inn has a long and honored history of service on the fur-trading route, connecting Montreal to Portland, Maine. Innkeeper Maureen Magee has the old inn key to prove it! It's this heartfelt tradition of caring that separates this inn from others.

In a food processor, puree the potatoes. Add the garlic puree, bread crumbs, lemon juice, salt, and black pepper and process until combined. While processing, drizzle the oil into the potato mixture until well mixed.

Transfer the mixture to a medium-sized bowl and stir in the scallions and olives. Serve at room temperature with the flat bread. Makes 2 cups.

YIELD: VARIABLE APPETIZER SERVINGS

This recipe was created by chef Russell Stannard.

RABBIT HILL INN
LOWER WATERFORD, VERMONT

Salsa Fresca

2 cloves garlic, chopped
3 green onions, chopped
1 fresh green chili pepper, seeded and
*   coarsely chopped*
1 tablespoon chopped white or yellow
*   onions*
1 tablespoon fresh lime juice
2 large firm tomatoes, peeled and
*   coarsely chopped, or 3 canned plum*
*   tomatoes*
¹/₄ cup chopped fresh cilantro
Salt and freshly ground black pepper
*   to taste*

Channel Road Inn

This charming little inn, located a couple of blocks from the Pacific Ocean, is entirely staffed by women who devote extraordinary care to their enterprise. This wonderful place exudes such hospitality and friendliness, you feel more like a family member than an overnight guest.

In a blender on low speed, blend together the garlic, green onions, chili pepper, onions, and lime juice until well combined.

Scrape the blender and add the tomatoes, cilantro, salt, and black pepper. Blend for 2 to 5 seconds. (Tomatoes should be chunky not pureed.) Serve with blue corn chips or crackers. Makes 1 ¹/₂ to 2 cups.

YIELD: VARIABLE APPETIZER SERVINGS

CHANNEL ROAD INN
SANTA MONICA, CALIFORNIA

Cheese Straw Daisies

8 ounces sharp cheddar cheese, grated
¹/₂ cup vegetable shortening
¹/₂ cup (1 stick) butter
¹/₄ teaspoon cayenne pepper
1 teaspoon salt
1 tablespoon water
¹/₃ cup grated Parmesan or Romano
* cheese*
2 rounded cups all-purpose flour,
* sifted*
1 teaspoon baking powder

Mainstay Inn & Cottage

Some people might shy away from the idea of opening an inn in the heart of Cape May's historic district and in the center of a veritable bevy of inns, but not Tom and Sue Carroll. This one-time gambling club has been so meticulously restored that you can almost see the robber barons of a different era playing poker in the parlor. Serve Sue's *Cheese Straw Daisies* at your next party, and your guests will think your party was catered!

Preheat oven to 350° F. In a food processor, blend the cheddar cheese. Add the shortening and butter and blend again. Add the cayenne pepper, salt, and water and blend again. Add the Parmesan cheese, then add the flour and baking powder, one-third at a time, blending for a few seconds between each addition.

Stuff a cookie shooter with the mixture and using a star tip, divide the daisies (1 to 1¹/₂ tablespoons each) onto a large baking sheet. Bake for 10 to 15 minutes. Let cool and serve. Makes 70 to 80 small daisies.

YIELD: VARIABLE APPETIZER SERVINGS

MAINSTAY INN & COTTAGE
CAPE MAY, NEW JERSEY

CHAPTER 3

Soups, Salads & Sides

Vegetable Vomacka

2 tablespoons butter or margarine
1/2 cup chopped onions
1/2 cup chopped carrots
1/2 cup chopped celery
2 cloves garlic, finely chopped
2 tablespoons all-purpose flour
3 cups chicken stock
1 tablespoon instant chicken bouillon
  granules
1 teaspoon dried dill
1 1/2 teaspoons pickling spice
1/4 teaspoon black peppercorns
1 1/2 teaspoons chopped fresh green
  beans
1 1/2 cups peeled diced potatoes
1 cup whipping cream
2 to 3 teaspoons cider vinegar

Schumacher's New Prague Hotel

Rarely do we encounter a well-run inn that is owned and managed by a person who is equally comfortable and adept at greeting guests at the front door and also at preparing a smooth and scintillating hollandaise in the kitchen. John Schumacher and his wife Kathleen balance the act beautifully. The *Vegetable Vomacka* is unusual and splendid!

In a large, heavy pot or Dutch oven, melt the butter and sauté the onions, carrots, celery, and garlic on medium-high heat for 4 to 6 minutes, or until the vegetables are tender, but not browned. Reduce heat to medium. Stir in the flour and cook, stirring constantly, for 2 minutes. (Do not brown.)

Stir in the chicken stock, bouillon granules, and dill. Tie the pickling spice and peppercorns in a small cheesecloth bag and add to the soup. Bring to a slow, rolling boil. Reduce heat to simmer and cook, covered, for 20 minutes. After 10 minutes, add the beans. Cover and simmer for 10 minutes more.

Add the potatoes and return to a boil. Reduce heat to simmer and cook for 15 minutes.

Remove spice bag. Slowly stir in the cream, then add the vinegar. Serve.

YIELD: 4 TO 6 SERVINGS

SCHUMACHER'S NEW PRAGUE HOTEL
NEW PRAGUE, MINNESOTA

Yellow Tomato Soup with Fresh Thyme & Yogurt

1 tablespoon olive oil
2 medium onions, finely chopped
2 cloves garlic, finely chopped
2 to 3 sprigs fresh thyme
4 pounds (8 large) yellow tomatoes, chopped
1 cup chicken stock
1 cup heavy cream
2 cups plain yogurt
Salt and freshly ground black pepper to taste

In a large saucepan, heat the oil and sauté the onions and garlic for 3 to 5 minutes, or until the onions are translucent. Stir in the thyme, tomatoes, and chicken stock and bring to a boil. Reduce heat to simmer and cook for 30 minutes. Remove the thyme sprigs.

In a blender or food processor, puree the soup, in batches, and strain out the tomato skins. Return the soup to the saucepan. Mix in the cream and yogurt and bring to a boil. Remove from heat and add the salt and pepper. Serve immediately.

YIELD: 6 SERVINGS

SILVER THATCH INN
CHARLOTTESVILLE, VIRGINIA

Szechuan Carrot Soup

1 teaspoon vegetable oil
1 medium onion, chopped
1 stalk celery, chopped
1 clove garlic, finely chopped
3 cups chicken stock
1 pound carrots, peeled and cut into
   1-inch rounds
One ³/₄-inch length fresh gingerroot,
   peeled and sliced
1 teaspoon dried red pepper flakes
1¹/₂ tablespoons soy sauce
1¹/₂ tablespoons peanut butter
2 teaspoons granulated sugar
1 teaspoon sesame oil

Manchester Highlands Inn

Featherbeds, down comforters, and a cat named Humphrey will be among your top ten favorite things after one visit to this grand Victorian inn, perched atop a hill overlooking Manchester, Vermont.

1 cup skim milk
Salt and freshly ground black pepper
   to taste
¹/₂ cup sour cream
2 tablespoons heavy cream

In a large pot, heat the vegetable oil and sauté the onion, celery, and garlic for 5 minutes or until soft. Add the chicken stock, carrots, gingerroot, and pepper flakes and bring to a boil. Reduce heat to simmer and cook for 45 minutes, or until the carrots are very tender. Stir in the soy sauce, peanut butter, sugar, sesame oil, and milk.

In a blender or food processor, puree the soup, in batches, until very smooth. Return the soup to the pot and heat through. Add the salt and black pepper.

In a small bowl, mix together the sour cream and heavy cream until smooth and thin. Pour the mixture into a squeeze bottle. Ladle the soup into soup bowls and with the bottle, make a pinwheel design in the center of each serving of soup. Then take a toothpick and pull through the pinwheel from the center out to form a spiderweb design. Serve immediately.

YIELD: 6 TO 8 SERVINGS

MANCHESTER HIGHLANDS INN
MANCHESTER CENTER, VERMONT

Mountain Apple & Vidalia Soup with Aged Gruyère & Parmesan Cheeses

2 cups beef stock
3 cups apple cider
1 bay leaf
1 teaspoon fresh thyme leaves
1 teaspoon coarsely ground black
  pepper
Salt to taste
3 tablespoons butter
2 pounds 8 ounces Vidalia onions,
  thinly sliced

1 teaspoon salt
1 teaspoon granulated sugar
1 1/2 to 2 tablespoons sherry
24 large garlic croutons
1/2 cup grated Parmesan cheese
1/2 cup grated Gruyère cheese
1 cup diced chilled North Carolina
  red apples
Fresh chives, chopped

In a large pot, combine the first six ingredients and bring to a gentle boil. Reduce heat to simmer and cook for 1 hour.

In a large skillet, melt the butter and sauté the onions for 3 to 5 minutes. Add the 1 teaspoon salt and the sugar and sauté for 4 to 5 minutes more, or until the onions are browned and thoroughly cooked. Deglaze the skillet with the sherry and add the onion mixture to the cider mixture. Simmer for 1 hour.

Ladle the soup into small, ovenproof soup bowls and top each serving with 3 garlic croutons. Divide both cheeses among the servings and place the bowls in the oven. Brown under the broiler for 1 to 2 minutes. Garnish with the diced apples and the chives and serve immediately.

YIELD: 8 SERVINGS

RICHMOND HILL INN
ASHEVILLE, NORTH CAROLINA

Pumpkin Soup

1 tablepoon butter
1 large onion, diced
2 pounds 8 ounces diced fresh pumpkin, or 3 cups pumpkin puree
6 cups chicken stock
3 tablespoons all-purpose flour
¹/₂ teaspoon salt
¹/₄ cup chopped fresh parsley
Croutons

In a large saucepan, melt the butter and sauté the onion for 4 to 6 minutes or until golden. Mix in the pumpkin and chicken stock and cook on medium heat for 10 minutes.

Remove 1 cup of the liquid and whisk in the flour. Return the flour mixture to the soup and cook, stirring occasionally, for 5 minutes. Stir in the salt and parsley. Serve immediately with the croutons.

YIELD: 8 SERVINGS

CASTLE MARNE
DENVER, COLORADO

Chicken & Andouille Sausage Gumbo

One 2-pound chicken, cooked, skinned, and deboned; reserve 8 cups stock
2 large onions, chopped
1/2 bunch celery, chopped
1/4 cup chopped green onions
1/4 cup chopped red bell peppers
3 pounds fresh okra, cut into 1/2-inch pieces
1/4 cup chopped fresh parsley
1 tablespoon filé powder
1 tablespoon seasoning salt
1/2 cup brown gravy
1 pound smoked pork or beef sausage, cooked and drained

In a large pot, combine the reserved chicken stock, onions, celery, green onions, bell peppers, okra, parsley, filé powder, salt, and gravy and cook on medium heat, stirring frequently, for 1 hour.

Add the cooked chicken and the sausage and cook for 15 to 20 minutes more. Adjust the seasonings. Serve immediately.

YIELD: 6 TO 8 SERVINGS

MADEWOOD PLANTATION HOUSE
NAPOLEONVILLE, LOUISIANA

Ham Hock Consommé with Fava & Lima Beans

Stock:

3 pounds ham hocks

3 tablespoons olive oil

2 medium carrots, chopped

2 stalks celery, chopped

1 large onion, chopped

1 large leek, well washed, trimmed, and chopped

1 head garlic, cut in half

1 bay leaf

1 small bunch fresh parsley

3 sprigs fresh thyme

1/2 cup sherry

5 black peppercorns

1 tablespoon tomato paste

4 quarts water

Consommé:

2 large carrots, chopped

3 stalks celery, chopped

2 medium onions, chopped

3 cloves garlic, peeled

1 pound ground sirloin beef

1 bay leaf

5 black peppercorns

8 egg whites

2 whole cloves

Salt and freshly ground black pepper to taste

Beans:

2 cups ham hock stock

1 cup dried fava beans

1 cup dried lima beans

6 bay leaves

Preheat oven to 350° F. To make the stock: In an uncovered roasting pan, brown the ham hocks for 45 minutes.

In a large pot, heat the oil and sauté the carrots, celery, onion, leek, and garlic for 7 to 10 minutes or until browned.

Add the roasted ham hocks, bay leaf, parsley, thyme, sherry, peppercorns, tomato paste, and water and slowly bring to a boil. Reduce heat to simmer and cook, uncovered, for 2 hours 30 minutes. Strain the stock and let cool. Remove the meat from the ham hocks and shred. Set the meat aside.

To make the consommé: In a food processor, grind the carrots, celery, onions, and garlic. Remove and combine with the remaining ingredients, except the salt and black pepper, in a large bowl.

In the large pot, combine the beef mixture with the strained and cooled stock and vigorously whisk together. Slowly bring the mixture to a point just below boiling without stirring. Reduce heat to simmer and gently cook the stock until the raft coagulates and rises to the top of the pot. Gently push the raft to the side to form a small crater through which the liquid can be seen. Once the raft has formed, simmer the consommé for 1 hour.

Gently strain the liquid through cheesecloth. Season with the salt and black pepper and keep warm.

To make the beans: In a medium-sized, heavy saucepan, heat the stock on medium-to-high heat and add the beans. Cook for 5 to 7 minutes or until tender but not mushy. Drain and set the beans aside.

To assemble the dish: Place 2 tablespoons of the reserved beans in each warm soup bowl. Add 2 tablespoons of the reserved shredded hock meat and 1 bay leaf. Ladle the consommé into each bowl and serve immediately.

YIELD: 6 SERVINGS

CARTER HOUSE/HOTEL CARTER
EUREKA, CALIFORNIA

Yellow Gazpacho with Avocado

10 medium yellow or orange tomatoes or combination, cored
3 yellow or orange bell peppers or combination, seeded and deveined
4 tablespoons fresh lime juice
1 1/2 tablespoons extra-virgin olive oil
Salt and freshly ground black pepper to taste
1/2 small white onion, finely chopped
1 ripe avocado, pureed
2 tablespoons melted butter
1/2 ficelle (thin loaf French bread), cut into rounds
1/2 cup loosely packed fresh cilantro leaves

Quarter all of the tomatoes and bell peppers, except 1 tomato and 1 bell pepper. In a food processor, puree the quartered tomatoes and bell peppers. Strain into a large bowl and discard solids. Stir in 3 tablespoons of the lime juice, the oil, salt, and black pepper. Cover and chill for several hours.

Just before serving, add the remaining lime juice, the onion, and pureed avocado. Spread the butter on the bread rounds and toast. Sprinkle the cilantro leaves over the top of the warm bread. Ladle the chilled soup in soup bowls and serve with the toasted bread.

YIELD: 8 SERVINGS

SIMPSON HOUSE
SANTA BARBARA, CALIFORNIA

Chilled Apple Soup with Sorrel & Yogurt

1 tablespoon butter
5 shallots, diced, or 1 medium onion, diced
1 medium leek, well washed and diced
4 Granny Smith apples, peeled and diced
1/2 cup chopped fresh sorrel
1/2 cup water or apple juice
1/2 cup buttermilk
1 1/2 cups plain yogurt
Salt and freshly ground black pepper to taste
Fresh cilantro, chopped

In a large saucepan, melt the butter and sauté the shallots and leek for 3 to 5 minutes or until translucent. Add the apples, sorrel, and water and simmer for 25 minutes.

In a blender or food processor, puree the apple mixture. Return the mixture to the saucepan and stir in the buttermilk and yogurt. Bring to a boil, then remove from heat *immediately* or separation will occur. Add the salt and black pepper and chill for 2 to 3 hours.

Garnish with the cilantro and serve immediately.

YIELD: 6 TO 8 SERVINGS

SILVER THATCH INN
CHARLOTTESVILLE, VIRGINIA

Strawberry Soup

15 ounces frozen strawberries,
   thawed with juice
15 ounces low-fat sour cream
1 tablespoon grenadine syrup
1 tablespoon pure vanilla extract
1 tablespoon pure rum extract
6 tablespoons sifted confectioners'
   sugar
1/4 cup half-and-half
3 large fresh strawberries, rinsed
   and halved

Country Goose Inn

Located only 12 miles from Memphis, Tennessee, this inn is described by innkeeper Callie Pfannenstiel as a comfortable and hospitable retreat from the distractions of daily life. On a hot, humid summer day, definitely prepare this *Strawberry Soup*. A cup of this thick and rich concoction will refresh your taste buds as nothing else can.

In a medium-sized bowl, combine the strawberries and sour cream and beat slowly until well mixed. Stir in the syrup, both extracts, and the sugar and mix until smooth. Add the half-and-half and mix only until blended. Chill for several hours.

Stir the soup before serving. Ladle into small soup bowls or cups and garnish each serving with 1 halved strawberry. Serve.

YIELD: 6 SERVINGS

COUNTRY GOOSE INN
MEMPHIS, TENNESSEE

Poached Salmon on Mixed Greens with Raspberry Vinaigrette

1 pound fresh salmon fillet
$^1/_2$ lemon, sliced
$^1/_3$ cup white wine
1 bay leaf
1 teaspoon salt
4 to 6 black peppercorns
Fresh endive lettuce leaves, rinsed
   and dried
Mixed fresh mesclun and watercress,
   rinsed and dried
1 recipe Raspberry Vinaigrette
(see recipe below)

In a poaching pan or shallow saucepan, place the salmon. Cover with water and add the lemon, wine, bay leaf, salt, and peppercorns. Bring to a simmer and poach for 15 minutes. Let cool in the water, then chill for 2 hours.

Remove the skin from the salmon and cut the salmon into chunks. Place the endive in star fashion on each salad plate and top with the mesclun and watercress. Place the salmon chunks on top and dot with the Raspberry Vinaigrette. Serve immediately.

YIELD: 6 SERVINGS

Raspberry Vinaigrette

1 cup raspberry vinegar
$^1/_3$ cup honey
2 tablespoons French grained mustard
1 tablespoon chopped fresh parsley
1 tablespoon granulated sugar
$1^1/_2$ cups vegetable oil
Salt and freshly ground black pepper
   to taste

In a food processor, combine the first five ingredients. While processing, slowly add the oil. Add the salt and black pepper. Makes $2^1/_2$ to 3 cups.

OLIVER LOUD'S INN/RICHARDSON'S CANAL HOUSE
PITTSFORD, NEW YORK

Marinated Crab & Fennel Salad with Roasted Red Pepper Sauce

*1 cup cleaned picked fresh Dungeness
    crabmeat*
1 cup diced fennel bulb
4 tablespoons extra-virgin olive oil
1 tablespoon cider vinegar
1 teaspoon fresh lemon juice

*Salt and freshly ground white pepper
    to taste*
1 recipe Garlic Croutons
    (see recipe below)
1 recipe Roasted Red Pepper Sauce
    (see recipe below)

In a medium-sized bowl, toss together the first six ingredients. Mound 1 tablespoon of the crab salad onto a warm *Garlic Crouton* and place on each salad plate.

Garnish with a small sprig of the fennel top and a small dollop of the *Roasted Red Pepper Sauce.* Serve immediately.

YIELD: 6 TO 8 SERVINGS

Garlic Croutons

2 heads garlic
1 cup extra-virgin olive oil
*Salt and coarsely ground black pepper
    to taste*
*1 slightly stale sourdough baguette,
    cut into rounds*

Preheat oven to 450° F. Peel off the loose papery covering on the outside of each garlic head and cut ¼ inch off the top to expose the garlic cloves. In a small bowl, immerse the garlic heads in the oil and let stand for about 10 minutes. Sprinkle with the salt and black pepper.

Place the garlic mixture in a baking pan and roast for 20 to 30 minutes, or until the cloves are soft and the oil starts to caramelize. Remove the cloves from the heads.

In a blender, blend the garlic cloves with the oil on low speed until just combined. Adjust the seasonings. Spread the mixture on the bread rounds and bake at 450° until lightly browned. Keep warm.

Roasted Red Pepper Sauce

1 medium red bell pepper
¼ cup dry white wine
2 whole scallions, finely chopped
1 clove garlic, finely chopped
1 cup heavy cream
Salt to taste
Dash freshly ground white pepper
Dash cayenne pepper

Roast the bell pepper whole under the broiler until the skin is darkened. Wrap in a wet paper towel for 5 to 10 minutes to steam the skin. Remove the skin.

In a food processor, puree the bell pepper. In a small saucepan, combine the wine, scallions, and garlic and reduce until approximately 1 tablespoon wine remains. Stir in the cream and reduce on medium heat until the mixture thickens. Add the salt and white and cayenne peppers. Add the cream mixture to the puree in the food processor and puree until well combined. Strain through a fine mesh sieve and set aside.

CARTER HOUSE/HOTEL CARTER
EUREKA, CALIFORNIA

Salad of Baby Greens with Brandied Apple & Fennel Top Vinaigrette with Crème Fraîche & Toasted Hazelnuts

Salad:

8 cups rinsed dried fresh mixed baby greens and lettuces

Extra-virgin olive oil

Salt and coarsely ground black pepper to taste

1 recipe Brandied Apple & Fennel Top Vinaigrette (*see recipe below*)

1 recipe Toasted Hazelnuts (*see recipe below*)

1 recipe Crème Fraîche (*see recipe below*)

To make the salad: Lightly toss 1 cup of the greens per serving in the oil, salt, and black pepper. Ladle 2 to 4 tablespoons of the *Brandied Apple & Fennel Top Vinaigrette* onto each serving plate and top with the greens mixture.

Sprinkle with the *Toasted Hazelnuts* and "paint" each plate with the *Crème Fraîche*. Serve immediately.

YIELD: 8 SERVINGS

Brandied Apple & Fennel Top Vinaigrette

1/2 cup peeled sliced Granny Smith apples

1/2 cup Calvados apple brandy

2 tablespoons chopped fresh fennel top

1 tablespoon Dijon mustard

1 1/2 tablespoons cider vinegar

Juice of 1/2 lemon

1/4 cup granulated sugar

1/2 cup olive oil

1/2 cup good-quality vegetable oil

Salt and freshly ground white pepper to taste

Carter House/Hotel Carter

Mark and Christi Carter are like the Hiltons of northern California innkeeping—only better! Just steps from the picturesque bay, which defines the western border of Eureka, these two facilities offer it all. When I am asked about "favorites," it is difficult to resist acknowledging Mark and Christi's kitchen garden as the most picturesque in the business.

In a small saucepan, stew the apples in the brandy on medium heat until tender. In a food processor, combine the warm apple mixture, the fennel, mustard, vinegar, lemon juice, and sugar and process until smooth. (If desired, the puree may be strained to produce a smoother product.)

With the processor at lowest speed, slowly drizzle in both oils, ¹/₄ cup at a time. (Do not overprocess, the desired result is an emulsion with a slight sheen.) Add the salt and white pepper. Makes about 2 cups.

Toasted Hazelnuts

2 cups shelled skinned hazelnuts

Preheat oven to 350° F. Spread the hazelnuts evenly on a baking sheet and roast for 20 minutes. Remove from oven and let cool.

Coarsely chop the cooled hazelnuts and set aside. Makes 2 cups.

Crème Fraîche

1 cup heavy cream, at room
temperature
2 tablespoons buttermilk, at room
temperature

In a warmed glass jar, combine the cream and buttermilk. Cover the jar securely and set in a warm place (approximately 75° F) for 8 to 10 hours.

Refrigerate when the mixture has thickened to the desired consistency. Makes 1 cup. (The crème fraîche can be stored for 8 to 10 days in the refrigerator.)

CARTER HOUSE/HOTEL CARTER
EUREKA, CALIFORNIA

Spring Festival Salad

6 cups rinsed dried ripped mixed
  fresh greens (romaine, endive,
  arugula, radicchio)
1/2 cup dried cranberries
1/2 cup raisins
1/2 cup roasted sliced almonds
1/2 cup crumbled Gorgonzola cheese
12 large grapefruit sections
4 large fresh strawberries, rinsed and
  sliced

The Inn at Olde Berlin/ Gabriel's

This fully restored Victorian home, built in 1906 by a wealthy Philadelphia merchant named Jacob Schoch, could be the flagship of the historic little town of New Berlin, Pennsylvania. Nancy and John Showers have become specialists at making their guests feel like family. Come and visit.

Place 1 1/2 cups of the mixed greens on each salad plate. Sprinkle 2 tablespoons of *each* of the next four ingredients on top of the greens.

Arrange 3 of the grapefruit sections in a spiral on top of the greens and fan 1 sliced strawberry in the center of the grapefruit sections. Serve with favorite salad dressing.

YIELD: 4 SERVINGS

THE INN AT OLDE BERLIN/GABRIEL'S
NEW BERLIN, PENNSYLVANIA

Ironrod Chèvre Dressing with Fresh Chives

1 cup balsamic vinegar
1 cup extra-virgin olive oil
1 tablespoon freshly ground black
  pepper
1/2 teaspoon kosher salt

1 tablespoon granulated sugar
1 cup chopped fresh chives
1 pound chèvre cheese, cut into small
  pieces
1/2 cup finely chopped onions

In a medium-sized bowl, whisk together all of the ingredients until creamy. Adjust the seasonings and serve.

YIELD: 4 CUPS

CLIFTON, THE COUNTRY INN
CHARLOTTESVILLE, VIRGINIA

Honey Dressing

1 cup vegetable oil
1/2 teaspoon salt
1 teaspoon ground mustard
1 teaspoon onion juice
1 tablespoon celery seeds
1 teaspoon ground paprika

1/3 cup honey
1/2 cup granulated sugar
5 tablespoons cider vinegar
1 tablespoon fresh lemon juice
1/2 cup white wine

In a blender or food processor, mix together all of the ingredients until well blended. Serve.

YIELD: ABOUT 2 1/2 CUPS

MONMOUTH PLANTATION
NATCHEZ, MISSISSIPPI

Molded Gazpacho Timbale

*3 envelopes unflavored powdered
  gelatin*
2 1/4 cups tomato juice
1/3 cup red wine vinegar
1/2 teaspoon salt
Dash Tabasco sauce
1 1/4 cups peeled seeded diced tomatoes
1 1/2 cups peeled diced cucumbers
1/2 cup chopped red bell peppers
4 whole scallions, finely chopped
1/2 cup chopped celery
*1 tablespoon chopped mixed fresh
  herbs (parsley, tarragon, chives)*

The Fearrington House

It's difficult not to like an inn that has become so popular it has spawned an entire village. A few minutes south of Chapel Hill, North Carolina, is one of only a handful of Relais et Chateaux country inns in the United States. We make it a point to visit chef Cory Mattson's kitchen every chance we get. Cory is remarkably adept at combining seemingly dissimilar ingredients to create a gastronomic blend that always pleases. His *Molded Gazpacho Timbale* is a terrific example of his handiwork!

In a large saucepan, sprinkle the gelatin over 1 cup of the tomato juice and heat on low heat, stirring constantly, until the gelatin dissolves. Remove from heat and blend in the remaining tomato juice, the vinegar, salt, and Tabasco sauce. Set in the refrigerator until the mixture is the consistency of unbeaten egg whites, stirring occasionally.

Fold the tomatoes, cucumbers, bell peppers, scallions, celery, and herbs into the chilled mixture. Rinse a 2-cup mold with cold water and pour the mixture into the mold. Chill for 6 hours or until firm. Unmold and serve immediately.

YIELD: 6 TO 8 SERVINGS

*THE FEARRINGTON HOUSE
PITTSBORO, NORTH CAROLINA*

Pureed Beets

Salt and freshly ground black pepper to taste
2 pounds fresh beets, scrubbed and trimmed
4 cups water
¼ cup prepared horseradish sauce
2 tablespoons red wine vinegar
¼ cup (½ stick) butter
Salt and freshly ground black pepper to taste

Preheat oven to 400° F. Sprinkle the salt and black pepper on the beets and place in a deep baking pan. Cover the beets with the water and bake, covered, for 1 hour 30 minutes, or until the beets are tender.

Peel the hot beets under cool, running water. In a food processor, combine the beets and remaining ingredients and process until smooth. In a large saucepan, heat the beet mixture until heated through. Serve immediately.

YIELD: 8 SERVINGS

CHESTERFIELD INN
WEST CHESTERFIELD, NEW HAMPSHIRE

Swiss Scalloped Potatoes

3 large potatoes, peeled and sliced
Salt and freshly ground black pepper
   to taste
Prepared mustard
4 ounces Swiss cheese, thinly sliced
3 medium onions, thinly sliced
¹/₄ cup bacon bits
¹/₂ cup dry vermouth
¹/₄ cup dried bread crumbs
¹/₄ cup grated Parmesan cheese
¹/₄ cup (¹/₂ stick) butter

Preheat oven to 350° F. In a buttered casserole dish, place a layer of the potatoes. Sprinkle on the salt and black pepper. Spread the mustard on the Swiss cheese slices and place a layer of the cheese slices on top of the potatoes. Layer the onions on top of the cheese and sprinkle with the bacon bits. Repeat layers until the dish is full.

Chalet Suzanne

When Carl and Bertha Hinshaw's land development partnership with cheese magnate J.L. Kraft went the way of many others in 1929, they decided to put their lifelong love for entertaining and travel to good use by opening an inn in Lake Wales, Florida. So in 1931, Chalet Suzanne (named after the Hinshaw's daughter) began operation. Today, more than 64 years and four generations of Hinshaws later, this popular destination has become a favorite of celebrities and vacationing families alike. Their Mobil Four-Star rating is a clear indication that a lot of people share our enthusiasm for this very special inn.

   Pour the vermouth over the top and sprinkle on the bread crumbs. Top with the Parmesan cheese and dot with the butter. Bake, covered, for 20 minutes. Uncover and allow top to brown. Bake, uncovered, for 10 minutes more. Serve immediately.

   YIELD: 6 TO 8 SERVINGS

CHALET SUZANNE
LAKE WALES, FLORIDA

Sweet Potato Casserole

3 cups mashed cooked sweet potatoes
1/2 teaspoon pure vanilla extract
1/2 cup (1 stick) butter, melted
1 cup granulated sugar
2 eggs, beaten
1/2 cup milk

Topping:
1 cup packed brown sugar
1/2 cup all-purpose flour
1/2 cup (1 stick) butter
1 cup chopped pecans

Grandview Lodge

Rarely do you come across a recipe for a dish that is as familiar as the comfort foods of your childhood. Stan and Linda Arnold's Grandview Lodge in Waynesville, North Carolina, gives you one of those comfort foods with this recipe for *Sweet Potato Casserole*. Try it and remember.

In a large bowl, beat together the first six ingredients and place the mixture in a lightly greased 9 x 13-inch baking pan. Set aside.

Preheat oven to 350° F. To make the topping: In a food processor, combine all of the ingredients and process until crumbly. Sprinkle the mixture over the reserved potatoes and bake, uncovered, for 45 to 50 minutes or until browned and bubbly. Serve immediately.

YIELD: 6 TO 8 SERVINGS

GRANDVIEW LODGE
WAYNESVILLE, NORTH CAROLINA

Gabriel's Stuffed Acorn Squash

1 to 2 tablespoons olive oil
1 1/2 cups chopped mixed fresh vegetables
  (broccoli, cauliflower, zucchini, summer squash, snow peas, scallions)
16 carrot rounds
16 fresh mushroom slices
1/2 teaspoon dried basil
1/2 teaspoon dried oregano
1/2 teaspoon dried thyme
Salt and freshly ground black pepper to taste
1 cup white wine
2 to 4 teaspoons fresh lime juice
2 acorn squash, halved, seeded, and steamed
4 to 8 teaspoons brown sugar
8 ounces Gouda cheese, grated

In a large, deep skillet, heat the oil and sauté all of the vegetables for 4 to 6 minutes or until tender-crisp. Stir in the herbs, salt, black pepper, wine, and lime juice and simmer for 3 to 4 minutes.

Preheat oven to 350° F. Coat the inside of each squash half with 1 to 2 teaspoons of the brown sugar and fill with the hot vegetable mixture. Top each squash half with 1/4 to 1/2 cup of the cheese and bake for 15 minutes or until heated through. Serve immediately.

YIELD: 4 SERVINGS

THE INN AT OLDE BERLIN/GABRIEL'S
NEW BERLIN, PENNSYLVANIA

Pumpkin La Fourche

2 pounds sweet potatoes, cooked and mashed
1 1/4 cups cooked mashed fresh pumpkin
3/4 cup granulated sugar
3 1/2 tablespoons golden raisins
8 ounces apples, peeled, sliced, and mashed
2 1/2 teaspoons pure vanilla extract
1/4 teaspoon ground cinnamon
1/4 teaspoon ground nutmeg
3 tablespoons softened margarine

Preheat oven to 325° F. In a large bowl, combine all of the ingredients and mix together well. Place the mixture in a greased casserole dish and bake for 30 minutes. Serve immediately.

YIELD: 6 TO 8 SERVINGS

MADEWOOD PLANTATION HOUSE
NAPOLEONVILLE, LOUISIANA

Baked Herb Polenta with Fresh Concasse of Tomato

2 quarts milk
³/₄ cup dried basil
¹/₂ teaspoon finely chopped garlic
¹/₂ teaspoon chicken stock
2 cups yellow cornmeal
¹/₂ cup grated Parmesan cheese
Salt and freshly ground black pepper
  to taste
Garlic powder to taste
1 large eggplant, cut into ¹/₄-inch
  slices
Olive oil
1 recipe Tomato Concasse
  (see recipe below)

To make the polenta: In a the stainless steel top of a large double boiler, heat the milk over hot water. Stir in the basil, garlic, and chicken stock. When the milk is scalded, slowly add the cornmeal, stirring constantly, until the mixture starts to thicken. Continue to add the cornmeal until a spoon stands up firmly in the mixture. Stir in the cheese, salt, black pepper, and garlic powder. Keep warm.

Lightly coat the eggplant slices with the oil and place on a baking sheet. Grill the slices under the broiler. Remove and let cool.

Preheat oven to 350° F. In a 12 x 15-inch greased baking pan, spread half of the polenta. Place the grilled eggplant evenly over the polenta. Top the eggplant layer with the remaining polenta and bake for 25 to 30 minutes or until golden brown. (Do not overbake.) Let cool for 5 to 10 minutes on a wire rack.

Top each serving of the warm polenta with the *Tomato Concasse* and serve immediately.

YIELD: 8 SERVINGS

Tomato Concasse

2 tablespoons vegetable oil
4 cups chopped tomatoes
$^{1}/_{2}$ cup finely chopped garlic
$^{1}/_{2}$ cup chopped fresh basil
$^{1}/_{2}$ teaspoon white wine
$^{1}/_{2}$ teaspoon fresh lemon juice

Salt and freshly ground black pepper
  to taste
Garlic powder to taste

In a large skillet, heat the oil and sauté the tomatoes, garlic, and basil for 5 to 10 minutes, or until the tomatoes are softened.

Stir in the wine, lemon juice, salt, black pepper, and garlic powder and heat through. Makes 4 cups.

THE 1661 INN/HOTEL MANISSES
BLOCK ISLAND, RHODE ISLAND

Baked Polenta

2 cups chicken stock
1 clove garlic, finely chopped
¹/₂ cup yellow cornmeal
2 tablespoons butter
¹/₄ cup shredded cheddar cheese
6 tablespoons grated Parmesan cheese
2 tablespoons butter, melted

The Gingerbread Mansion

The first time that we visited this impeccably detailed Victorian beauty, it was like a vision becoming reality. No wonder! This inn has graced the cover of more books, puzzles, and postcards than any other inn anywhere. Come for a visit and see for yourself.

In a large saucepan, combine the stock and garlic and bring to boil. Slowly add the cornmeal, stirring constantly. Reduce heat to a gentle boil and cook, stirring constantly, for 4 to 5 minutes, or until the mixture becomes thick and pulls away from the sides of the saucepan. Stir in the butter, cheddar cheese, and 4 tablespoons of the Parmesan cheese and mix together well.

Pour the mixture into a greased 9 x 5-inch loaf pan and let cool. Cover and chill overnight.

Preheat oven to 350° F. Remove the chilled polenta from the pan and cut into ³/₄-inch thick slices. Place overlapping slices in a greased, shallow casserole dish and drizzle the butter over the top. Sprinkle with the remaining Parmesan cheese and bake, uncovered, for 30 minutes. Serve immediately.

YIELD: 6 TO 8 SERVINGS

THE GINGERBREAD MANSION
FERNDALE, CALIFORNIA

Couscous with Chickpeas & Tomato

1 ¹/₂ cups chicken stock
2 tablespoons butter
1 cup uncooked couscous
1 medium tomato, seeded and diced
¹/₂ cup cooked chickpeas
¹/₄ cup raisins
¹/₄ teaspoon ground cinnamon
¹/₄ teaspoon crumbled dried basil
¹/₄ teaspoon crumbled dried thyme
Salt and freshly ground black pepper to taste

Preheat oven to 350° F. In a medium-sized, heavy saucepan, bring the stock and butter to a boil. Add the couscous. Reduce heat to simmer and cook, covered, for 5 minutes, or until the couscous is tender and the liquid is absorbed.

Stir in the remaining ingredients and place the mixture in a small, buttered baking pan. Bake, covered, for 15 minutes or until heated through. Serve immediately.

YIELD: 4 SERVINGS

ROSSWOOD PLANTATION
LORMAN, MISSISSIPPI

Apricot Chutney

1 tablespoon vegetable oil
1 large onion, chopped
1 tablespoon peeled grated fresh
  gingerroot
1 tablespoon mustard seeds
1 teaspoon curry powder
$^1/_8$ teaspoon cayenne pepper
2 cups coarsely chopped dried apricots
$^2/_3$ cup golden raisins
$^1/_2$ cup white vinegar
$^1/_3$ cup granulated sugar
Salt to taste
$^1/_3$ cup chopped fresh cilantro

Old Monterey Inn

There is a lot of beauty to behold on California's Monterey Peninsula. But if you visit Monterey just for the pier, you are missing the real jewel in the crown of this popular bayside village. Ann and Gene Swett not only prepare and serve a memorable *Apricot Chutney*, but also are widely acknowledged by innkeeping insiders as the king and queen of California innkeeping and for a very good reason. This inn sets the standards by which others are measured.

In a 3-quart, nonstick skillet, heat the oil and sauté the onion and gingerroot for 4 to 6 minutes, or until the onion is lightly browned. Stir in the mustard seeds, curry powder, and cayenne pepper and sauté, stirring constantly, for 4 minutes. Mix in the remaining ingredients, except the salt and cilantro, and cook for 7 minutes.

Stir in the salt and cilantro. Remove from heat and let cool. Serve with roasted meats, poultry, or Indian curries.

YIELD: ABOUT 2 CUPS

OLD MONTEREY INN
MONTEREY, CALIFORNIA

CHAPTER 4

Entrées

Roast Peppered Rib Eye of Beef

¹/₄ cup coarsely ground black pepper
One 2- to 3-pound rib eye beef roast, fat removed
¹/₂ teaspoon ground paprika
¹/₂ cup soy sauce
¹/₃ cup red wine vinegar
¹/₂ tablespoon tomato paste
¹/₂ tablespoon cornstarch
¹/₄ teaspoon garlic powder

Rub the black pepper over the roast and press in with heel of hand. Place the roast in a shallow baking pan. In a jar with a tight-fitting lid, combine the remaining ingredients and shake well. Carefully pour the mixture over the roast and marinate overnight in the refrigerator.

Preheat oven to 325° F. Remove the roast from the marinade and bake for 17 to 20 minutes *per pound* for rare. (For the best results, use a meat thermometer.) Let cool slightly. Slice and serve immediately.

YIELD: 4 TO 6 SERVINGS

ROSSWOOD PLANTATION
LORMAN, MISSISSIPPI

Medallions of Beef Atlanta Bleu

3 to 4 tablespoons butter
Six 6-ounce beef tenderloin medal-
lions
6 tablespoons burgundy wine
6 tablespoons heavy cream
3 tablespoons crumbled bleu cheese
Seasoned salt to taste
Freshly ground black pepper to taste
Crumbled bleu cheese
Fresh parsley, chopped

In a large skillet, melt the butter and sauté the medallions. Deglaze the skillet with the wine. Stir in the cream and cheese and reduce by half as the cheese melts. Add the salt and black pepper.

Remove the medallions when cooked to choice. Pour the sauce over the meat and sprinkle with more cheese and the parsley. Serve immediately.

YIELD: 6 SERVINGS

Tara—A Country Inn

In all our travels, we know of only one elegant country inn that is thematically devoted to Tara, the epitome of the southern plantation home in the film *Gone with the Wind*. These inspired innkeepers have even collected original costumes from the film to accessorize their rooms. Their attention to detail, however, does not stop with decor. Jim and Donna Winner appreciate fine food, and they insist upon serving their guests creatively and generously. The *Medallions of Beef Atlanta Bleu* will convert even the most dedicated fish or fowl aficionado.

TARA—A COUNTRY INN
CLARK, PENNSYLVANIA

Pear Wood Smoked Tenderloin of Veal with Poached Pear, Sun-Dried Tomato & Grilled Shiitake Mushroom Vinaigrette

One 2-pound veal tenderloin
Salt and freshly ground black pepper
  to taste
Granulated sugar to taste
1 1/2 tablespoons vegetable oil
1 cup pure maple syrup
1/2 tablespoon vegetable oil
1/2 cup diced fresh shiitake mushrooms
2 cups white wine

6 sun-dried tomatoes, soaked and
  diced
4 Bartlett pears, peeled, halved
  lengthwise, and cored
1/4 cup diced shallots
2 tablespoons chopped fresh chives
1/4 cup raspberry vinegar
1/4 cup water
Salt and freshly ground black pepper
  to taste
8 fresh shiitake mushrooms, grilled

Clifton, The Country Inn

In bucolic Charlottesville, Virginia, chef/innkeeper Craig Hartman and his wife Donna go the extra step for their guests every day of the week, every week of the year. The attention and service at this beautiful historic inn manage to excite the palate, nurture the senses, and pamper the soul—all at the same time. Craig's *Pear Wood Smoked Tenderloin of Veal* was the hit of the "Inn Country USA" festive Holiday Special.

Season the tenderloin with the salt, black pepper, and sugar. In a large, heavy skillet, heat the 1 1/2 tablespoons oil and sear the tenderloin on all sides. Place in a large, deep bowl and marinate in the syrup for at least 1 hour.

Remove the tenderloin and smoke over pear wood embers for 15 minutes, or until the meat is rare to medium rare. Slice and return the meat to the maple syrup and let cool in the refrigerator.

In a small skillet, heat the 1/2 tablespoon oil and lightly sauté the mushrooms. Remove the mixture and grill for

30 to 45 seconds. Set aside.

To poach the pears: In a large saucepan, combine the pear halves and wine and bring to a boil. Reduce heat to simmer and cook, covered, for 15 minutes or until just tender. Fan four of the pear halves and set aside. Dice the remaining pears and place in a large bowl. Add the tomatoes, reserved mushroom mixture, shallots, chives, vinegar, water, salt, and black pepper and mix together well. Adjust the seasonings.

Place a ladle of the vinaigrette in the center of each serving plate, then place on each plate 2 slices of the veal, 1 pear fan, and 2 grilled mushrooms. Serve immediately.

YIELD: 4 SERVINGS

CLIFTON, THE COUNTRY INN
CHARLOTTESVILLE, VIRGINIA

Grilled Veal Loin Chops Stuffed with Brie & Scallions

1 bunch scallions, chopped
1 pound Brie cheese, at room temperature
Eight 8-ounce veal loin chops
Olive oil
Salt and freshly ground black pepper to taste

In a medium-sized bowl, combine the scallions and cheese and mash into a soft paste. Cut a pocket in the side of each chop, making a slit to the bone. Fill each chop with the scallion paste.

Preheat the grill or broiler. Brush each chop with the oil and season with the salt and black pepper. Cook the chops for about 3 minutes on each side. (Veal chops should remain slightly pink in the center.) Serve immediately.

YIELD: 8 SERVINGS

CHESTERFIELD INN
WEST CHESTERFIELD, NEW HAMPSHIRE

Veal with B and B & Blueberries

1 cup chicken stock
$^{1}/_{2}$ cup B and B liqueur
$^{3}/_{4}$ cup dried blueberries
1 teaspoon chopped fresh thyme
$^{1}/_{2}$ teaspoon ground allspice
Four 5- to 6-ounce veal fillets,
  pounded to $^{1}/_{4}$-inch thickness
Seasoned flour
2 tablespoons butter
2 medium shallots, finely chopped
$^{3}/_{4}$ cup heavy cream
4 sprigs fresh thyme
Edible flower blossoms

The Governor's Inn

In every industry there are leaders — people who make it their business to set an example for their peers. Whether it's hosting a cooking school weekend, baking a mile-high apple pie, being quoted on the back of 20 million rice boxes, or collecting antique knife rests, Charlie and Deedy Marble spend a lot of time trying out new and better ways to pamper the people that they serve at their little Victorian inn at the foot of Okemo Mountain.

In a small nonreactive saucepan, mix together the first five ingredients. Cover and simmer for 8 minutes, until the blueberries have plumped. Set aside.

Dredge the veal in the seasoned flour and shake off all excess. In a large, deep skillet, melt the butter on medium heat and sauté the fillets until browned, turning once. Remove the fillets and keep warm.

Add the shallots to the skillet and sauté for 1 minute. Deglaze the skillet with the reserved blueberry mixture and bring to a boil. Stir in the cream, reduce heat to simmer, and cook, stirring constantly, for 4 minutes, or until the mixture is of sauce consistency.

Spread the sauce on the bottom of each serving plate and place slices of the warm veal on top of the sauce. Garnish each plate with 1 sprig of thyme and the flowers.

YIELD: 4 SERVINGS

THE GOVERNOR'S INN
LUDLOW, VERMONT

Rack of Venison with Spiced Cranberry & Black Bean Sauce

1 recipe Spiced Cranberry & Black
　Bean Sauce (*see recipe below*)
1 rack venison roast
1 tablespoon dried oregano
1 tablespoon dried thyme
1 tablespoon ground cumin
¹/₂ tablespoon ground coriander
³/₄ teaspoon ground nutmeg
*1 tablespoon freshly ground black
　pepper*
1 pound (4 sticks) unsalted butter
10 whole green onions, trimmed
10 cloves garlic, peeled
³/₄ cup merlot red wine

Beaufort Inn

Few southern coastal towns can lay
claim to the silver screen exposure that
has been enjoyed by Beaufort, South
Carolina. If the set designer said, "I
need an inn that looks like it belongs,"
she would no doubt end up at Rusty
and Debbie's place. Here are two
bright entrepreneurs who have managed to open an inn with the patina of
a place that has been there forever.

Preheat oven to 350°F. French the
bones of the fat around the eye of the
roast. In a small bowl, mix together all
of the herbs and spices and rub the
mixture twice on the outside of the
roast.

In a large, cast-iron Dutch oven,
melt the butter. When the Dutch oven
is hot, place the roast in the bottom and
surround with the onions and garlic.
Sauté each side of the roast for about 3
minutes.

Add the wine and bake for about 15
minutes for medium rare. (Venison
should not be cooked more than medium
rare or may loose significant amount of
flavor.) Let cool slightly. Serve with the
Spiced Cranberry & Black Bean Sauce.

YIELD: 4 TO 6 SERVINGS

Spiced Cranberry & Black Bean Sauce

1 pound fresh cranberries
¹/₂ cup white or apple vinegar
1 cup packed dark brown sugar
2 teaspoons ground cinnamon
¹/₂ teaspoon ground cloves

2 Granny Smith apples, cored and
   chopped
Grated peel of 1 orange
1 pound cooked black beans
5 tablespoons chopped fresh cilantro
Salt and freshly ground black pepper
   to taste

In a large saucepan, combine the first seven ingredients and bring to a boil. Reduce heat to simmer and cook for 30 minutes.

Stir in the remaining ingredients and heat through. Keep warm. Makes about 3 cups.

BEAUFORT INN
BEAUFORT, SOUTH CAROLINA

Roast Loin of Pork with Apple-Walnut Coulis

One 2¹/₂- to 3-pound boneless pork
　loin, split
1 recipe Apple-Walnut Coulis
　(see recipe below)
¹/₄ cup olive oil
Salt and coarsely ground black pepper
　to taste
¹/₂ cup water
¹/₂ cup dark sweet sherry or pure
　maple syrup
¹/₂ cup golden raisins

Preheat oven to 275° F. Wash the pork loin in cool water and pat dry. Stuff the pork with ¹/₂ cup of the *Apple-Walnut Coulis* in the split. Tie the loin back together and rub with the oil. Sprinkle with the salt and black pepper.

Place the loin on a wire rack in a large baking pan and roast for 50 to 60 minutes. (Insert a meat thermometer and check to be sure 160° has been reached before removing the roasted loin.) Remove from oven and let stand for 15 minutes.

Meanwhile, deglaze the bottom of the pan with the water and reduce. Stir in the sherry and raisins and reduce until slightly thickened.

Divide the sauce among the serving plates. Slice the pork and fan out the

Adams Edgeworth Inn

This inn is in the middle of a gated community that is essentially a year-round, chautauqua-style village. David and Wendy Adams are a couple of worldly folks with colorful backgrounds, rich memories, and a genuine need to share their lives with other people. Nowhere is Wendy's gift for sharing more evident than when she turns her attention to the kitchen.

slices over the sauce. Divide the remaining coulis and place beside the pork. Serve immediately.

　YIELD: 4 TO 6 SERVINGS

Apple-Walnut Coulis

¹/₄ cup (¹/₂ stick) butter
3 cups peeled chopped apples
¹/₂ cup packed brown sugar
¹/₂ cup dark sweet sherry
¹/₂ cup golden raisins
¹/₄ cup chopped walnuts

In a large saucepan, melt the butter and

cook the apples on medium heat until tender. Add the sugar, stirring constantly, to avoid scorching. Stir in the sherry. Add the raisins and walnuts and mix together until well combined. Makes 3 $\frac{1}{2}$ to 4 cups.

ADAMS EDGEWORTH INN
MONTEAGLE, TENNESSEE

Pork Tenderloin Wrapped in Pancétta with Parmesan Crackers & Sun-Dried Polenta

Polenta:
3/4 cup water
1/2 cup yellow cornmeal
1 1/4 cups chicken stock
3/4 cup grated Parmesan cheese
1/4 cup julienned sun-dried tomatoes
2 tablespoons heavy cream
2 tablespoons butter
Salt and freshly ground black pepper
   to taste
1 recipe Beurre Blanc
   (see recipe below)
1 recipe Parmesan Crackers
   (see recipe below)

Pork:
2 tablespoons Dijon mustard
Four 3-ounce center-cut pork
   tenderloins
Salt and freshly ground black pepper
   to taste
4 slices pancétta

Leeks:
1 cup safflower oil
1/2 cup finely julienned leeks
1/4 cup all-purpose flour

Shrimp:
1/4 cup (1/2 stick) butter
12 large shrimp (10 to 15 count),
   peeled and deveined with tails
1/2 cup coarsely chopped endive lettuce
1/2 cup chopped leeks
1 teaspoon finely chopped garlic
Salt and freshly ground black pepper
   to taste

To make the polenta: In a small bowl, stir together the water and cornmeal. In a medium-sized saucepan, bring the stock to a boil and slowly add the cornmeal mixture, stirring constantly, until well blended. Reduce heat to simmer and cook, stirring frequently, until thick. Mix in the cheese, tomatoes, cream, butter, salt, and black pepper. Transfer the mixture to four 3-inch metal cooking rings set on a baking sheet and chill.

Preheat oven to 350° F. To make the pork: Spread the mustard on the tenderloins and season with the salt and black pepper. Wrap the loins with the pancétta and hold in place with toothpicks. Heat a large, ovenproof sauté pan and sear the loins. Bake for 12 to 15 minutes. Keep warm.

To make the leeks: In a large saucepan, heat the oil to 375° F. Lightly dust the leeks with the flour and deep-fry until crisp. Drain on paper towels and set aside.

To make the shrimp: In a large skillet, melt the butter and sauté the shrimp for 2 to 3 minutes. Remove the shrimp and keep warm. Add the remaining ingredients and sauté until tender. Set aside.

Preheat oven to 350° F. Bake the chilled polenta for 10 to 15 minutes or until heated through. Ladle 2 tablespoons of the vermouth *Beurre Blanc* around each serving plate. Squeeze 7 dots of the mustard *Beurre Blanc* onto the vermouth sauce and gently swirl together with a toothpick.

In the center of each plate, place the endive mixture and center 1 warm polenta cake on top of the endive mixture. Place 1 *Parmesan Cracker* on top of the polenta and place the pork pancétta on the cracker. Add a second cracker on top of the pork and arrange a few fried leeks on top of the cracker. Place 3 shrimp around the edge of each plate and serve immediately.

YIELD: 4 SERVINGS

Beurre Blanc

6 tablespoons ($^1/_4$ stick) butter
3 shallots, chopped
1 clove garlic, finely chopped
$^1/_2$ cup dry vermouth
3 cups heavy cream
$^2/_3$ cup butter
3 tablespoons prepared grainy
  mustard

In a large saucepan, melt the 6 tablespoons butter and sauté the shallots and garlic for 3 to 5 minutes or until tender. Deglaze the saucepan with the vermouth. Stir in the cream and reduce by half. Whisk in the $^2/_3$ cup butter and stir until melted.

In a food processor, place the cream mixture and process until smooth. Reserve half of the sauce and blend in the mustard. Place both sauces in squeeze bottles and keep warm.

Parmesan Crackers

4 sheets phyllo pastry
$^1/_4$ cup melted butter
6 tablespoons grated Parmesan cheese

Preheat oven to 350° F. Brush 1 sheet of the pastry with the butter and sprinkle on the cheese. Repeat the procedure, stacking each sheet on top of the previous one, until four layers are complete.

With a 3-inch round cutter, cut 8 circles from the layers. Line a rimmed baking sheet with parchment paper and place the circles on the parchment. Cover with a second sheet of parchment paper and place another baking sheet on top of the first to weigh down the pastry. Bake for 10 to 12 minutes or until golden brown and crisp. Set aside.

JOSEPHINE'S BED & BREAKFAST
SEASIDE, FLORIDA

Rolled Stuffed Pork Tenderloin with Arugula Pesto

1 tablespoon olive oil
1 clove garlic, finely chopped
1 small bunch fresh spinach (8 to 10 ounces), rinsed and trimmed
One 2- to 3-pound pork tenderloin, split and pounded
Salt and freshly ground black pepper to taste
1 roasted red bell pepper, skinned, seeded, and cut into strips
2 tablespoons grated fontina cheese
2 tablespoons pine nuts
Flour
3 eggs, lightly beaten with 6 tablespoons water
Olive oil
Fresh bread crumbs
1 recipe Arugula Pesto (see recipe below)

In a medium-sized skillet, heat the oil and sauté the garlic for 3 to 5 minutes. Add the spinach and sauté for 3 to 5 minutes more. Set aside.

Preheat oven to 400° F. Sprinkle the loin with the salt and black pepper. Spread the split tenderloin with the re-served spinach mixture, bell pepper strips, cheese, and pine nuts. Roll up the stuffed tenderloin and roll in the flour, then in the egg wash. Coat with the bread crumbs.

Place the loin in a preheated, large, oiled baking pan and brown on all sides. Roast for 15 to 20 minutes, or until a meat thermometer reads 160°. Remove from oven and let stand for 10 to 15 minutes. Slice and serve with the *Arugula Pesto.*

YIELD: 4 TO 6 SERVINGS

Arugula Pesto

1 small bunch fresh arugula lettuce
1/4 cup cornichons (gherkins)
3 tablespoons capers
3 tablespoons pine nuts
1/2 cup olive oil
2 tablespoons grated Romano cheese

In a food processor, process the arugula, cornichons, capers, and pine nuts. Keep processing and slowly pour in the oil and add the cheese. Makes about 3/4 cup.

THE RHETT HOUSE INN
BEAUFORT, SOUTH CAROLINA

Lavender & Mint Roasted Pork Tenderloin

Pork:
Three 12-ounce pork tenderloins
1/4 cup finely chopped fresh lavender
3/4 cup finely chopped fresh mint
Sweet butter

Chutney:
1 cup dried cherries
2 fresh persimmons, thinly sliced
6 dried figs, thinly sliced
1/2 medium red bell pepper, seeded,
    deveined, and julienned
1/2 medium green bell pepper, seeded,
    deveined, and diced
Juice of 1/2 lemon
1 teaspoon peeled grated fresh ginger-
    root
2 cloves garlic, finely chopped
1/4 cup white wine vinegar
1/2 cup gewürztraminer wine
Pinch cayenne pepper
Salt and freshly ground black pepper
    to taste

Caramelized Apples:
2 tablespoons sweet butter
3 Granny Smith apples, cored and
    sliced
1/4 cup packed brown sugar
2 tablespoons cider vinegar

Pumpkin Mixture:
1 pound fresh pumpkin, seeded
1 pound white turnips, peeled and
    quartered
2 tablespoons butter, melted
1/2 cup grated Asiago cheese
1/4 to 1/2 cup heavy cream
1 clove garlic, finely chopped
1 teaspoon ground nutmeg

To make the pork: Trim any excess fat and silverskin from the tenderloins and discard. In a large, shallow bowl, combine the lavender and mint. Roll the tenderloins in the herbs to thoroughly coat the meat. Cover and refrigerate overnight.

To make the chutney: In a medium-sized, heavy saucepan, combine all of the ingredients and bring to a boil. Reduce heat to simmer and cook, stirring frequently, for 1 to 1 hour 30 minutes, or until the chutney has stewed and the fruits and vegetables are tender. Let cool to room temperature and set aside.

To make the caramelized apples: In a hot skillet, brown the butter. Add the apple slices and toss. Add the sugar and continue to toss until the sugar begins to caramelize. Gently stir in the vinegar and cook on low heat, stirring frequently, until the liquid reduces to a light syrup. Keep warm.

Preheat oven to 350° F. To make the pumpkin mixture: Place the pumpkin in a baking pan and bake for 30 to 40 minutes or until tender.

Meanwhile, in a medium-sized saucepan, cook the turnips in water to cover for 20 minutes or until tender. Drain and mash the turnips. Set aside.

Scrape the meat of the cooked pumpkin into a large bowl and stir in the butter. Mix in the reserved mashed turnips. Add the cheese, cream, garlic, and nutmeg and mash the mixture to a smooth consistency. Keep warm.

Preheat oven to 350° F. In a large, heavy ovenproof skillet, melt enough of the sweet butter to cover the bottom. When the butter is hot, brown the chilled pork tenderloins on both sides. Bake for 15 minutes, or until the pork is cooked to medium. Remove and let stand for 5 minutes.

Slice the pork on a bias and arrange on each serving plate with the chutney, caramelized apples, and pumpkin mixture. Serve immediately.

YIELD: 6 SERVINGS

CARTER HOUSE/HOTEL CARTER
EUREKA, CALIFORNIA

Roast Long Island Duckling with Cranberry Glaze

One 5¹/₂- to 6-pound Long Island
　duckling
¹/₂ medium apple, peeled and diced
1 small onion, diced
¹/₈ large lemon, peeled, sectioned, and
　diced
¹/₄ medium orange, peeled, sectioned,
　and diced
2 bay leaves
Salt and freshly ground black pepper
　to taste
2 tablespoons honey
3 tablespoons soy sauce
Pinch ground ginger
1 recipe Cranberry Demi-Glace
　(see recipe below)

Preheat oven to 325° F. Spray the rack
of a roasting pan with vegetable spray.
Remove the neck and giblets from the
duck and trim off any excess skin and
fat. Rinse out the cavity and pat dry.

In a small bowl, combine the apple,
onion, lemon, orange, and bay leaves
and stuff the mixture into the duck cavity. Prick the top and sides of the duck
with a fork and season the skin with the
salt and black pepper. Place the duck in
the prepared pan and roast for 3 hours.

Remove from oven and drain off
the fat, reserving the fat for the *Duck
Espagnole.* Reduce temperature to 250°
and return the duck to the oven.

In a small bowl, mix together the
honey, soy sauce, and ginger. Roast the
duck for 10 minutes more, basting
twice with the honey mixture. Remove
and let cool slightly. Serve with the
Cranberry Demi-Glace.

YIELD: 4 SERVINGS

Cranberry Demi-Glace

¹/₄ cup granulated sugar
1 tablespoon fresh lemon juice
6 tablespoons cranberry juice
1 tablespoon currant jelly
¹/₄ cup Cointreau liqueur
4 cups Duck Espagnole
　(see recipe below)
One 12-ounce bag fresh cranberries

In a large, heavy saucepan, cook the
sugar on medium heat for 5 to 6 minutes, or until caramelizes and turns a
light brown color. (Do not burn.)

Remove from heat and stir in the remaining ingredients, except the cranberries. The caramel will harden, but stir the mixture together thoroughly and return to heat. Cook, stirring occasionally, on medium heat for 40 minutes or until reduced by one-third. Add the cranberries and boil for 5 to 6 minutes, or until the cranberries pop. Makes 2 ¹/₂ to 3 cups.

Duck Espagnole

¹/₄ cup reserved duck fat
¹/₂ medium onion, chopped
1 medium carrot, chopped
2 stalks celery, chopped
1 clove garlic, finely chopped
2 shallots, chopped
1 medium tomato, chopped
2 tablespoons tomato paste
2 bay leaves
1 teaspoon dried thyme
1 teaspoon freshly ground black
  pepper
1 teaspoon dried rosemary
8 cups chicken stock
1 cup (2 sticks) butter

1 cup all-purpose flour
Dash salt

In a large pot, heat the fat and sauté the next six ingredients for 30 minutes. Add the tomato paste, bay leaves, thyme, black pepper, and rosemary and cook for 10 minutes. Stir in the stock and simmer for 2 hours.

In a small saucepan, melt the butter. Stir in the flour and cook, stirring constantly, on medium heat for 2 to 3 minutes. Add the flour mixture to the stock and cook for 1 hour more, or until the sauce is thickened and reduced to 4 cups. Skim off fat and strain the sauce. Add the salt. Makes 4 cups.

The Red Lion Inn

Spend five minutes rocking on the front porch of this venerable old inn in Stockbridge, Massachusetts, and you will begin to feel like a Norman Rockwell model with an appetite! They do everything well here! Come and join us on the porch.

THE RED LION INN
STOCKBRIDGE, MASSACHUSETTS

Stuffed Free-Range Chicken Breasts with Lemon-Thyme Sauce

*Four 8-ounce free-range boneless
  chicken breasts*
8 ounces goat cheese, cut into 4 slices
8 ounces pancétta, cooked
1/2 cup corn kernels
*1 cup Lemon-Thyme Sauce
  (see recipe below)*
4 sprigs fresh lemon thyme

Preheat oven to 375° F. Spread the chicken breasts out flat, skin side down. Divide the cheese, pancétta, and corn equally in the centers of each breast and roll up each breast in a cylindrical shape. Place the stuffed breasts in a baking pan and bake for 10 minutes.

Ladle 2 to 4 tablespoons of the *Lemon-Thyme Sauce* into the center of each serving plate and coat each plate well. Slice each roulade of chicken into 5 rounds and place around the front center of the well of each plate.

Place 1 herb sprig just off center of each plate and serve immediately.

YIELD: 4 SERVINGS

Lemon-Thyme Sauce

4 cups chardonnay wine
4 shallots, finely chopped
4 bay leaves
1/2 cup white wine vinegar
*2 tablespoons chopped fresh lemon
  thyme*
1/2 cup heavy cream
3 pounds unsalted butter

In a large saucepan, stir together the first five ingredients on medium heat and reduce until nearly dry.

Remove from heat and add the cream. Reduce by half, then strain. Slowly whisk in the butter, in batches, until thickened. Keep warm.

*RICHMOND HILL INN
ASHEVILLE, NORTH CAROLINA*

Peach Salsa Chicken

1 tablespoon ground cumin
1 ¼ cups fresh orange juice
¼ cup olive oil
3 tablespoons hot chili powder
8 boneless skinless chicken breasts
2 small fresh green chilies or to taste,
  chopped
1 cup honey

1 cup chicken stock
4 medium fresh peaches, peeled and
  chopped
1 teaspoon finely chopped garlic
¼ cup diced onions
2 tablespoons chopped fresh chives
1 tablespoon peach schnapps

In a small bowl, whisk together the cumin, orange juice, oil, and 1 tablespoon of the chili powder. Arrange the chicken in a large, shallow dish and cover with the orange juice mixture, turning the chicken to coat well. Marinate, covered, in the refrigerator for at least 1 hour or overnight.

In a large saucepan, combine the remaining chili powder, the chilies, honey, stock, peaches, garlic, onions, chives, and schnapps and bring to a boil. Reduce heat to simmer and cook, stirring occasionally, for 30 minutes or until slightly thickened. Set aside.

Place the marinated chicken on an oiled rack set about four inches above hot coals and grill for 25 to 30 minutes or until cooked to choice, turning occasionally. Top each breast with the reserved salsa and serve immediately.

YIELD: 4 SERVINGS

THE INN AT OLDE BERLIN/GABRIEL'S
NEW BERLIN, PENNSYLVANIA

Spinach & Cheese Stuffing

25 ounces frozen spinach, cooked and well drained
¹/₄ cup (¹/₂ stick) butter
1 medium yellow onion, chopped
Pinch dried oregano
¹/₂ teaspoon dried thyme
1 tablespoon dried basil
1¹/₂ teaspoons finely chopped garlic
¹/₂ cup shredded cheddar cheese
¹/₃ cup grated Parmesan cheese
1 cup ricotta cheese
Salt and freshly ground black pepper to taste
¹/₄ cup dried bread crumbs
Garlic powder to taste

Place the cooked spinach in a large bowl and set aside. In a medium-sized skillet, melt the butter and sauté the onion and herbs for 3 to 5 minutes, or until the onion is translucent.

Add the onion mixture to the reserved spinach and mix together well. Stir in the remaining ingredients until well combined. Use for stuffing chicken.

YIELD: 6 TO 8 SERVINGS

MONMOUTH PLANTATION
NATCHEZ, MISSISSIPPI

Plantation Quail

8 semiboneless quail
2 tablespoons dried oregano
$^1/_4$ cup dried tarragon
2 tablespoons ground ginger
$^2/_3$ cup raspberry vinegar
2 tablespoons chopped garlic
$^1/_4$ cup freshly ground black pepper
$^1/_4$ cup pickling spice
3 cups olive oil
1 recipe Orange Sauce
  (see recipe below)

Remove the legs and wings at the joints, close to the bone, of each quail and place the remainder of each quail in a large, shallow bowl. In a medium-sized bowl, mix together the next eight ingredients and pour over the quail. Marinate in the refrigerator for 4 to 5 hours.

Remove the quail from the marinade and grill or sauté for 3 to 4 minutes for both sides. Divide the quail among the serving plates and top with the *Orange Sauce*. Serve immediately.

YIELD: 4 SERVINGS

Orange Sauce

4 cups chicken stock
1 cup red currant jelly
2 cups orange marmalade
4 tablespoons cornstarch
$^1/_2$ cup (1 stick) butter, melted
$^1/_2$ cup all-purpose flour

In a large saucepan, combine the stock, jelly, and marmalade and bring to a boil. Add the cornstarch, stirring constantly and return to a boil. Reduce heat to simmer and cook, stirring frequently, for 5 to 10 minutes.

Meanwhile, in a small saucepan, heat the butter and stir in the flour to make a roux the consistency of paste. Add the roux to the stock mixture, stirring constantly until smooth. Makes 5 to 6 cups.

THE GREYSTONE INN
LAKE TOXAWAY, NORTH CAROLINA

Breast of Pheasant

Four 5-ounce pheasant breasts
  (4 half breasts)
1 cup Apricot-Pistachio Nut Stuffing
  (see recipe below)
4 cups seasoned all-purpose flour
¹/₄ cup egg wash
2 teaspoons sage-seasoned dried
  bread crumbs
1¹/₂ cups Red Currant & Citrus
  Brandy Glaze *(see recipe below)*
4 teaspoons diced dried apricots
4 teaspoons chopped pistachio nuts
4 sprigs fresh herbs

Richmond Hill Inn

This inn is perched like a crown jewel on a crest in the Blue Ridge Mountain town of Asheville, North Carolina. When "Inn Country USA" visited this 1889 Queen Anne mansion, we were looking forward to sampling some of chef John Babb's innovative dishes. One taste of the *Breast of Pheasant* with *Apricot-Pistachio Nut Stuffing* convinced us that we love this place!

Preheat oven to 350° F. Pound each breast until thin and tender. Spread ¹/₄ cup of the chilled *Apricot-Pistachio Nut Stuffing* evenly across each breast and roll up in pinwheel fashion. Roll lightly in the flour and dip in the egg wash. Then roll each breast in the bread crumbs and place in a baking pan. Roast for 8 to 10 minutes or until golden brown.

In the center of each serving plate, ladle 6 tablespoons of the warm *Red Currant & Citrus Brandy Glaze.* Slice each roasted breast into five "rounds" and overlap the rounds on top of the glaze. Sprinkle 1 teaspoon of the apricots around the edge of the well of each

plate. Sprinkle the nuts around the edge of the well and on top of the apricots. Garnish each plate with 1 herb sprig. Serve immediately.

YIELD: 4 SERVINGS

Apricot-Pistachio Nut Stuffing

2 cups finely chopped dried apricots
6 tablespoons apricot brandy
¹/₂ cup heavy cream
2 eggs, beaten
4 cups cubed white bread
  (crust removed)
³/₄ cup finely chopped pistachio nuts
4 shallots, finely chopped

2 tablespoons chopped fresh parsley
1 tablespoon dried sage
1 stalk celery, finely chopped
¹/₂ teaspoon salt
¹/₂ teaspoon freshly ground black pepper
1 teaspoon poultry seasoning

In a large bowl, soak the apricots in the brandy until rehydrated. In a separate bowl, mix together the cream, eggs, and bread cubes and add to the apricot mixture. Mix in the remaining ingredients until well combined. Chill.

Red Currant & Citrus Brandy Glaze

4 cups water
3 cups granulated sugar
2 cups dried red currants
6 tablespoons apricot brandy
¹/₂ cup fresh orange juice
¹/₄ cup fresh lemon juice
1 cup (2 sticks) softened unsalted butter
Grated peel of 1 orange
Grated peel of 1 lemon

In a large saucepan, combine the water and sugar and cook for 1 hour or until syrupy and smooth. Add the currants and brandy and cook for 15 minutes. Whisk in both juices. Stir in the butter and whisk until smooth and shiny.

In a food processor, puree the mixture. Transfer the glaze to a large glass bowl and place in a water bath. Stir in the citrus zests. Keep warm. Makes 3 cups.

RICHMOND HILL INN
ASHEVILLE, NORTH CAROLINA

Pan-Seared Lobster over Wilted Greens with Sweet Red Pepper-Mango Marmalade

*Four 1-pound 8-ounce fresh Maine
  lobsters*
5 tablespoons clarified butter
*Salt and freshly ground black pepper
  to taste*
4 cups cooked buttered white rice
*1 recipe Sweet Red Pepper-Mango
  Marmalade (see recipe below)*
1 recipe Fritters (see recipe below)

Greens:
1 medium onion, sliced
2 strips bacon, julienned
*8 ounces fresh mustard greens,
  chopped into 1-inch pieces*
*8 ounces fresh Swiss chard, chopped
  into 1-inch pieces*
1 teaspoon balsamic vinegar
*Salt and freshly ground black pepper
  to taste*

Silver Thatch Inn

The Silver Thatch Inn is in good company. Just a few minutes from this award-winning Albemarle County inn are the homes of three presidents, Thomas Jefferson's Monticello, James Madison's Montpelier, and Ash Lawn, the former home of James Monroe. In fact, Virginia has been the birthplace of so many presidents, The Silver Thatch named each of its seven guest rooms after Virginia-born Presidents of the United States.

In a lobster pot, steam the lobsters for 10 minutes or until three-fourths cooked. Remove and let cool.

To make the greens: In a medium-sized saucepan, sauté the onion and bacon on medium heat for 3 to 5 minutes, or until the onion is translucent. Add all of the greens and cook, stirring constantly, until the greens are wilted. Stir in the vinegar, salt, and black pepper. Remove from heat and drain. Keep warm.

Remove the meat from each cooled lobster shell, keeping as much of the meat intact. Just before serving, in a large skillet, melt the butter and sauté the lobster meat until heated through. Season with the salt and black pepper.

Place 1 cup of the cooked rice in the center of each serving plate and divide the warm greens over the rice. Place the sautéed body and claw meat of 1 lobster on top of the greens. Ladle the *Sweet Red Pepper-Mango Marmalade* onto each plate around the rice (do not cover the lobster). Garnish each plate with the *Fritters* and serve immediately.

YIELD: 4 SERVINGS

Sweet Red Pepper-Mango Marmalade

1 cup granulated sugar
1 1/2 cups white vinegar
6 tablespoons frozen orange juice
  concentrate
1 medium onion, diced
4 medium-to-large red bell peppers,
  seeded, deveined, and chopped
1 ripe mango, peeled and diced

In a large saucepan, mix together the sugar, vinegar, and concentrate and bring to a boil. Reduce heat to simmer and cook until reduced by half. Add the onion and bell peppers and cook, covered, for 30 minutes, or until the bell peppers are very tender.

In a blender or food processor, puree the bell pepper mixture. Return the mixture to the saucepan and stir in the mango. Keep warm.

Fritters

1 cup all-purpose flour
1/4 teaspoon salt
1/4 teaspoon freshly ground black
  pepper
1/2 cup beer
1 medium red bell pepper, seeded,
  deveined, and diced
1 small onion, diced
1/4 cup fresh or frozen corn kernals

In a medium-sized bowl, mix together the flour, salt, black pepper and beer to form a very thick batter. Let stand for 45 minutes. Add the remaining ingredients and stir vigorously until well combined.

Spoon the batter into 375° F oil and deep-fry to form small fritters. Remove the fritters from the oil and drain on paper towels. Keep warm. Makes 8 to 10 fritters.

SILVER THATCH INN
CHARLOTTESVILLE, VIRGINIA

Shrimp with Apple & Snow Peas in Wine & Mustard Cream Sauce

1 cup (2 sticks) butter
64 to 80 medium fresh shrimp (21 to 30 count), peeled and deveined
1/4 cup chopped garlic
1/4 cup chopped shallots
2/3 cup Riesling wine
2 cups crème fraîche
1/2 cup prepared grainy mustard
40 snow peas, trimmed and blanched

40 slices red apples, cut 1/4 inch thick
1 pound 8 ounces fettuccine pasta, cooked and drained
1/2 teaspoon dried oregano
1/2 teaspoon dried basil
Salt and freshly ground black pepper to taste
8 sprigs fresh dill
8 lemon slices

In a large saucepan, melt 1/2 cup of the butter and sauté the shrimp and 1 tablespoon *each* of the garlic and shallots for 1 to 2 minutes. Stir in the wine, crème fraîche, and mustard and simmer for 5 minutes. Keep warm.

In a large skillet, melt the remaining butter and sauté the remaining garlic and shallots for 2 to 3 minutes. Add the cooked pasta and heat through. Mix in the herbs, then add the salt and black pepper.

Divide the pasta mixture on serving plates and top clockwise with alternating 8 to 10 warm shrimp, 5 snow peas, and 5 apple slices per plate. Drizzle the remaining shrimp sauce over all and place 1 dill spring and 1 lemon slice on each plate. Serve immediately.

YIELD: 8 SERVINGS

RICHMOND HILL INN
ASHEVILLE, NORTH CAROLINA

Low-Country Boil

6 to 8 quarts water
1/2 teaspoon cayenne pepper
1 teaspoon whole cloves
2 cloves garlic, chopped
6 bay leaves
1 tablespoon Old Bay Seasoning
4 medium carrots, halved
2 pounds kielbasa or turkey kielbasa,
  cut into 1 1/2-inch pieces
2 small onions, quartered
16 new potatoes, scrubbed
8 ears fresh corn, shucked
2 pounds medium fresh shrimp
  (21 to 30 count) in shell
16 blue crabs in shell (optional)

Little St. Simons Island Inn

Twice daily, scheduled boat service transports the intrepid inngoer to this 10,000-acre, privately owned island retreat and to a place called serenity. Guided nature tours by jeep or horse and decidedly unguided strolls along a deserted seven-mile beach help to work up an appetite for a traditional *Low-Country Boil.*

In a very large steam kettle or outdoor fish cooker, bring the water to a boil. Season the water with the cayenne pepper, cloves, garlic, bay leaves, and Old Bay Seasoning.

Add the carrots, sausage, onions, and potatoes and boil for 7 to 10 minutes, or until the vegetables are almost tender. Add the ears of corn and boil for 3 to 4 minutes.

Reduce heat to simmer. Add the shrimp and crabs and cook for 3 to 4 minutes more or until just cooked. Serve immediately.

YIELD: 8 SERVINGS

LITTLE ST. SIMONS ISLAND INN
ST. SIMONS ISLAND, GEORGIA

Seafood Fettuccine

12 large fresh shrimp (16 to 20 count), peeled and deveined
12 fresh sea scallops (20 to 30 count), rinsed
12 ounces fresh lump crabmeat
4 tablespoons olive oil
2 medium tomatoes, blanched, chopped, and seeded
20 fresh basil leaves, chopped
2 teaspoons chopped garlic
4 cups heavy whipping cream
Salt and freshly ground black pepper to taste
12 ounces cooked fettuccine pasta
Fresh basil, chopped
Fresh parsley, chopped

In a large, hot skillet, sear the shrimp, scallops, and crabmeat for 1 minutes 30 seconds on each side. Remove from the skillet and keep warm.

Heat the oil in the same skillet and sauté the tomatoes, basil, and garlic for 3 to 5 minutes. Stir in the cream and reduce until thick. Add the salt and black pepper. Stir in the cooked pasta and heat through.

Divide the pasta mixture among the serving plates and top with the reserved warm shrimp mixture. Garnish with the basil and parsley and serve immediately.

YIELD: 4 SERVINGS

TARA—A COUNTRY INN
CLARK, PENNSYLVANIA

*RECIPES FROM RABBIT HILL INN, LOWER WATERFORD, VERMONT.
CLOCKWISE FROM TOP: SOUFFLÉD ORANGE-ALMOND CUSTARD;
MONKFISH WITH SWEET POTATO-HAZELNUT CRUST; SKORDALIA.*

ONION TARTS.
1842 INN, MACON, GEORGIA.

*RACK OF VENISON WITH SPICED CRANBERRY & BLACK BEAN SAUCE.
BEAUFORT INN, BEAUFORT, SOUTH CAROLINA.*

SMOKED SHENANDOAH TROUT MOUSSE
WITH DILL VIN BLANC SAUCE.
PROSPECT HILL PLANTATION INN,
TREVILIANS, VIRGINIA.

IRONROD CHÈVRE DRESSING WITH FRESH CHIVES.
CLIFTON, THE COUNTRY INN, CHARLOTTESVILLE, VIRGINIA.

Recipes from Silver Thatch Inn, Charlottesville, Virginia.
Clockwise from top: Chilled Apple Soup with Sorrel & Yogurt;
Pan-Seared Lobster over Wilted Greens with Sweet Red
Pepper-Mango Marmalade.

VEAL WITH B AND B & BLUEBERRIES.
THE GOVERNOR'S INN, LUDLOW, VERMONT.

LEEK & CHEDDAR TART WITH ROASTED RED PEPPER SAUCE.
THE DARBY FIELD INN, CONWAY, NEW HAMPSHIRE.

GABRIEL'S STUFFED ACORN SQUASH.
THE INN AT OLDE BERLIN/GABRIEL'S,
NEW BERLIN, PENNSYLVANIA.

ROAST LONG ISLAND DUCKLING WITH CRANBERRY GLAZE.
THE RED LION INN, STOCKBRIDGE, MASSACHUSETTS.

RECIPES FROM THE FEARRINGTON HOUSE, PITTSBORO, NORTH CAROLINA.
CLOCKWISE FROM TOP: BAKED MUSHROOMS STUFFED WITH COUNTRY SAUSAGE;
MOLDED GAZPACHO TIMBALE.

SALMON CAKES WITH POACHED EGGS & CREAMY DILL SAUCE.
THE MANSAKENNING CARRIAGE HOUSE, RHINEBECK, NEW YORK.

RECIPES FROM MAINSTAY INN & COTTAGE, CAPE MAY, NEW JERSEY.
CLOCKWISE FROM TOP: CHEESE STRAW DAISIES; BUTTER ALMOND CAKE.

DECADENT BREAD.
HERLONG MANSION, MICANOPY, FLORIDA.

VEGETABLE TULIP CUPS.
THE WHITEHALL INN, NEW HOPE, PENNSYLVANIA.

MARY'S STICKY BUNS.
MANOR HOUSE, CAPE MAY, NEW JERSEY.

CAPPUCCINO MUFFINS.
OLIVER LOUD'S INN/RICHARDSON'S CANAL HOUSE,
PITTSFORD, NEW YORK.

CRAIG HAMMELL

BITTERSWEET CHOCOLATE SOUFFLÉS WITH
WHITE CHOCOLATE & RUM SAUCE.
THE NEWCASTLE INN, NEWCASTLE, MAINE.

CRAIG HAMMELL

EGGNOG CHEESECAKE.
RICHMOND HILL INN, ASHEVILLE, NORTH CAROLINA.

Spectacular Strawberry Trifle.
The Queen Victoria, Cape May, New Jersey.

Red Snapper with Julienned Vegetables

2 tablespoons butter
Six 4-ounce fillets fresh red snapper
¼ teaspoon salt
Freshly ground white pepper to taste
2 shallots, finely chopped
12 sprigs fresh lemon thyme
2 cups julienned mixed vegetables (carrots, yellow squash, zucchini,
  red bell peppers)
3 ounces fresh snow peas, cut into diagonal pieces
6 tablespoons white wine
1 large lemon, cut into 6 slices

Cut six 9 x 12-inch pieces of parchment paper and six 6-inch lengths of string.

Preheat oven to 400° F. Cut the butter into thin shavings and divide among the pieces of the parchment paper. Place each fillet on top of the butter, skin side down, and season with the salt and white pepper. Sprinkle the shallots and lemon thyme over the fillets and surround with the julienned vegetables and snow peas. Pour 1 tablespoon of the wine over each fillet and top with 1 lemon slice.

Completely enclose the fillets in the parchment paper by loosely rolling up the paper. Fold the ends and use the strings to tie the ends together like a handle. (Do not tear the paper.) Bake for 15 to 20 minutes.

Place 1 parchment pocket on each serving plate and cut open. Serve immediately.
YIELD: 6 SERVINGS

THE FEARRINGTON HOUSE
PITTSBORO, NORTH CAROLINA

Beet Butter Sauce

¹/₂ cup white wine
¹/₂ cup white wine vinegar
1 shallot, finely chopped
1 medium fresh beet, cooked and
  grated
1 bay leaf
12 whole black peppercorns
1 cup (2 sticks) unsalted butter
2 tablespoons heavy cream

The Rhett House Inn

When we first saw the photograph of this inn in *The Innkeepers' Register*, we knew it had to be part of "Inn Country USA." The sweeping veranda of this 1820 plantation house makes it very tempting to remain outside, but Steve and Marianne Harrison have succeeded in making the inside of their inn every bit as inviting as the outside.

In a small saucepan, combine the wine and vinegar and reduce to 2 tablespoons liquid. Set aside.

In a separate saucepan, combine the shallot, beet, bay leaf, peppercorns, and butter and cook on low heat for 10 to 15 minutes, or until the mixture is well combined.

Add the reserved wine mixture. Stir in the cream and mix together well. Serve warm with baked red snapper or other white fish of choice.

YIELD: ABOUT 1 CUP

THE RHETT HOUSE INN
BEAUFORT, SOUTH CAROLINA

Crispy Southern Flounder with Peach Sauce

Four 12-ounce fresh southern flounders, cleaned and heads removed
Kosher salt
3 to 4 cups peanut or corn oil
2 cups rice flour
2 tablespoons finely chopped green
onions

Sauce:
1 tablespoon corn oil
1 tablespoon peeled grated fresh
gingerroot

1 tablespoon finely chopped garlic
1 1/2 cups chopped fresh or thawed
frozen peaches
1 teaspoon chopped fresh mint
1 teaspoon chopped fresh cilantro
1 teaspoon chopped fresh lemongrass
1 teaspoon finely chopped fresh
jalapeño pepper
One 15-ounce jar peach jam
2/3 cup oriental fish sauce*
1 teaspoon tamarind concentrate*
1/2 teaspoon garlic-chili sauce*

Wash and pat dry the flounders. Score both sides of each fish with a sharp knife in a diagonal pattern. Salt the fish with the kosher salt and set aside. In a large, deep skillet or wok, begin to heat the oil.

To make the sauce: In a large saucepan, heat the oil and sauté the gingerroot and garlic for 3 to 5 minutes. Stir in the remaining ingredients and simmer.

Dredge the reserved flounders in the flour and fry in the hot oil for 4 minutes or until lightly browned and crispy. Drain on paper towels.

Place 1 flounder on each serving plate and top with the warm sauce. Garnish with the green onions and serve immediately.

YIELD: 4 SERVINGS

Items are available in specialty shops and Asian markets.

LITTLE ST. SIMONS ISLAND INN
ST. SIMONS ISLAND, GEORGIA

Grilled Salmon Crusted with Hazelnuts with Shiitake Mushroom, Pear & Applejack Compote

Four 6- to 8-ounce fresh salmon
  fillets
4 tablespoons canola oil
Salt and freshly ground black
  pepper to taste

¹/₂ cup hazelnuts, roasted and
  crushed
1 recipe Shiitake Mushroom,
  Pear & Applejack Compote
  (see recipe below)

Brush each fillet with 1 tablespoon of the oil and season with the salt and black pepper. Grill to preferred doneness, then generously coat each fillet with the hazelnuts.

   Place the coated fillets on serving plates and top with the *Shiitake Mushroom, Pear & Applejack Compote.* Serve immediately.

   YIELD: 4 SERVINGS

Shiitake Mushroom, Pear & Applejack Compote

2 tablespoons canola oil
¹/₄ medium onion, sliced
One 1¹/₂-ounce package shiitake
  mushrooms, stemmed and sliced

1 semifirm Bosc pear, peeled and diced
¹/₄ cup applejack brandy
Salt and freshly ground black pepper
  to taste

In a medium-sized skillet, heat the oil and sauté the onion for 3 to 5 minutes or until translucent. Add the mushrooms and pear and sauté until the mushrooms wilt.

   Remove from heat. Pour in the brandy and return to heat. The mixture will flare, but the flame will burn out when the alcohol has evaporated. Cook for 1 minute more, then add the salt and black pepper. Keep warm.

Silver Thatch Inn
Charlottesville, Virginia

Monkfish with Sweet Potato-Hazelnut Crust

2 eggs, beaten
6 tablespoons ground hazelnuts
Four 6-ounce fresh monkfish fillets
Salt and freshly ground black pepper to taste
Flour
1 cup peeled grated raw sweet potatoes
½ cup olive oil

In a large, shallow bowl, stir together the eggs and hazelnuts and set aside.

Season the fillets with the salt and black pepper and dredge in the flour, then roll in the reserved egg mixture. Roll the fillets in the grated sweet potatoes and set aside.

Preheat oven to 350° F. In a large skillet, heat the oil until hot and sauté the reserved coated fillets until brown on both sides. Place the fillets in a baking pan and bake for 15 minutes or until firm to the touch. Serve immediately.

YIELD: 4 SERVINGS

This recipe was created by chef Russell Stannard.

RABBIT HILL INN
LOWER WATERFORD, VERMONT

Rainbow Trout Stuffed with Crab & Spinach

12 ounces fresh spinach, rinsed,
  trimmed, and shredded
1 medium onion, finely chopped
One 6-ounce can crabmeat
Dash ground thyme
1/2 tablespoon cayenne pepper
1/2 tablespoon Worchestershire sauce
2 cloves garlic, finely chopped
Pinch dried tarragon
1 tablespoon bacon fat
1 tablespoon cognac brandy
1 1/2 teaspoons sherry
1 1/2 teaspoons Pernod liqueur
Four 10-ounce (after cleaned and
  boned) trout with heads
1/4 cup (1/2 stick) butter
1/2 cup Hollandaise Sauce
  (see recipe below)
Red or yellow cavier
Lemon wedges

In a medium-sized bowl, combine the first eight ingredients and set aside.

Preheat oven to 375° F. In a medium-sized saucepan, melt the fat and stir in the brandy, sherry, and liqueur. Add the spinach mixture and cook until the moisture is absorbed.

Lay each trout skin side down and spread one-fourth of the spinach mix-

Castle Marne

The Peiker family and their "castle" are arguably the center of the inn-keeping universe in Denver, Colorado. Jim and Diane enjoy the distinction of having the smallest, although one of the most prolific kitchens in the entire "Inn Country USA" television series. This is *the* place to "do an inn" in the mile-high city.

ture on one side of the trout and fold together. Place the butter in the bottom of a shallow baking pan and place the fish on top of the butter. Bake for 15 to 20 minutes, or until the fish feel springy to the touch.

Place each trout on a serving plate and drizzle the *Hollandaise Sauce* over the top. Garnish with the cavier. Serve immediately with the lemon wedges.

YIELD: 4 SERVINGS

Hollandaise Sauce

3 egg yolks, beaten
1/4 cup water

2 tablespoons fresh lemon juice
8 tablespoons cold butter, divided

In a medium-sized saucepan, mix together the eggs, water, and lemon juice and cook, stirring constantly, until the mixture begins to thicken.

Whisk in the butter, 1 tablespoon at a time, and continue to cook until the butter is melted and the sauce is thickened.

CASTLE MARNE
DENVER, COLORADO

Black Bass with Red Chili Vinaigrette

Four 1-pound whole black bass,
  cleaned
1 recipe Red Chili Vinaigrette
  (see recipe below)
1 recipe Seasoned Bulgur Wheat
  (see recipe below)

Preheat oven to 375° F. Brush each bass
with ⅓ cup of the *Red Chili Vinaigrette*
and place belly side down on a large,
greased rimmed baking sheet. Bake for
20 minutes, or until the fish are flaky.
Serve immediately on a bed of the *Seasoned Bulgur Wheat.*

   YIELD: 4 SERVINGS

Red Chili Vinaigrette

¼ cup fresh lemon juice
1 cup olive oil
6 tablespoons apple cider vinegar
4 to 6 fresh red chili peppers
  (mild to medium hot), ground
1 habanero chili pepper, chopped

1 teaspoon freshly ground black
  pepper
1 tablespoon finely ground sea salt

In a medium-sized bowl, combine all of
the ingredients and mix together well.
Makes about 1½ cups.

Seasoned Bulgur Wheat

2 cups cooked bulgur wheat
1 pound 8 ounces fresh lump
  crabmeat, sautéed
4 tablespoons olive oil
½ cup roasted pine nuts
6 tablespoons chopped fresh parsley
2 tablespoons chopped fresh
  cilantro
1 pound chorizo sausage, chopped
  and cooked (optional)

In a medium-sized bowl, combine all of
the ingredients and mix together until
well combined. Makes 4 servings.

GREYFIELD INN
CUMBERLAND ISLAND, GEORGIA

Tomato-Basil Fettuccine with Wild Mushrooms

4 quarts water
2 tablespoons salt
1 pound 4 ounces fresh tomato–basil fettuccine pasta
6 tablespoons virgin olive oil
2 tablespoons finely chopped shallots
2 tablespoons finely chopped garlic
2 pounds fresh wild mushrooms (shiitake, enoki, blue oyster), trimmed and sliced
4 Italian plum tomatoes, peeled, seeded, and diced
1 cup dry white wine
1/2 cup chopped fresh herbs (basil, rosemary, oregano)
3/4 cup grated Asiago cheese
Salt and freshly ground black pepper to taste

In a large pot, bring the water to a rapid boil and add the 2 tablespoons salt. Add the pasta and cook for 4 to 5 minutes or until tender but still firm. Drain and set aside. Keep warm.

In a large skillet, heat the oil and sauté the shallots and garlic for 2 minutes. Add the mushrooms and sauté until the mushrooms start sweating. Stir in the tomatoes and wine and simmer for 3 minutes.

Add the reserved warm pasta and toss. Add the herbs and 1/2 cup of the cheese and toss lightly to combine. Add the salt and black pepper.

Divide the pasta mixture among serving plates and garnish with the remaining cheese. Serve immediately.

YIELD: 4 SERVINGS

CARTER HOUSE/HOTEL CARTER
EUREKA, CALIFORNIA

CHAPTER 5

Breads & Muffins

Lemon-Cheese Braid

1 tablespoon active dry yeast
¼ cup very warm water
  (110° to 115°F)
½ cup scalded milk
¼ cup granulated sugar
½ teaspoon salt
¼ cup (½ stick) softened butter
2 eggs, beaten
3 to 4 cups all–purpose flour

Filling:
12 ounces cream cheese
½ cup granulated sugar
1 egg, beaten
1 teaspoon grated lemon peel
½ cup raisins

Icing:
1 tablespoon butter, melted
½ cup confectioners' sugar
2 tablespoons fresh lemon juice

Romeo Inn

If you are the kind of creative soul who yearns to try recipes that are honest to goodness prize winners, try the Romeo Inn's inspired *Lemon-Cheese Bread.* Margaret Halverson is understandably proud to have won the First Prize at the Ashland Association of the Oregon Bed & Breakfast Guild.

In a small bowl, dissolve the yeast in the warm water. In a large bowl, mix together the milk, sugar, salt, butter, eggs, dissolved yeast, and 2 cups of the flour. Add the remaining flour, ½ cup at a time, until the dough is workable. Knead the dough, adding more flour to prevent sticking, until smooth and elastic. Place the dough in a greased bowl, cover with a towel, and let rise until doubled, about 1 hour.

To make the filling: In a medium-sized bowl, beat the cream cheese until soft. Gradually add the sugar and mix together well. Add the egg and lemon zest and stir until well combined. Mix in the raisins and set aside.

To make the icing: In a small bowl, mix together all of the ingredients and beat until smooth. Set aside.

Punch down the dough and roll into a 12 x 14-inch rectangle. Place the formed dough on a greased baking sheet and spread the reserved filling down the center-third of the dough. Cut the sides into 1-inch strips. Fold the strips over the filling, alternating from side to side, to form a braid. Cover with a towel and let rise until doubled, about 45 minutes.

Preheat oven to 375°F. Bake for 25 to 30 minutes. Immediately remove the bread from the baking sheet and cool on a wire rack. Drizzle with the reserved icing and serve.

YIELD: 1 LARGE LOAF

ROMEO INN
ASHLAND, OREGON

Lemon Bread

¹/₃ cup cooled melted sweet butter
1 cup granulated sugar
3 tablespoons pure lemon extract
2 large eggs, beaten
Grated peel of 1 large lemon
1¹/₂ cups sifted unbleached all-purpose flour
1 teaspoon salt
1 teaspoon baking powder
¹/₂ cup whole milk
¹/₂ cup chopped pecans

Topping:
Juice of 1 large lemon
¹/₂ cup confectioners' sugar

Preheat oven to 350° F. Butter a 9 x 5-inch loaf pan and line the bottom with wax paper. In a medium-sized bowl, mix together the first five ingredients. In a large bowl, stir together the flour, salt, and baking powder. Add the butter mixture and milk to the flour mixture and mix together well. Fold in the pecans. (Do not overmix.)

Pour the batter into the prepared pan and bake for 50 to 55 minutes.

To make the topping: In a small bowl, mix together the lemon juice and sugar and set aside.

Remove the baked bread from the pan and peel off the wax paper. Slowly pour the topping over the top of the bread until all of the liquid is soaked into the bread. Serve warm.

YIELD: 1 LOAF

VICTORIAN INN ON THE PARK
SAN FRANCISCO, CALIFORNIA

Blueberry Bread

½ cup (1 stick) butter, softened
1 cup granulated sugar
2 eggs
½ teaspoon pure vanilla extract
1 cup sour cream
2 cups all-purpose flour
1 teaspoon baking powder
1 teaspoon baking soda
1 cup fresh or thawed frozen blueberries

Preheat oven to 350° F. In a large bowl, cream the butter and sugar with an electric mixer. Beat in the eggs, vanilla, and sour cream. Mix in the flour, baking powder, and baking soda. Slowly fold in the blueberries.

Pour the batter into a greased 9 x 5-inch loaf pan and bake for 1 hour, or until a tester inserted in the center comes out clean. Let cool on a wire rack. Serve.

YIELD: 1 LOAF

CHANNEL ROAD INN
SANTA MONICA, CALIFORNIA

Pumpkin Bread

1 cup raisins
1 cup vegetable oil
3 eggs, beaten
One 16-ounce can pumpkin puree
2 1/2 cups granulated sugar
3 1/2 cups all-purpose flour
1/2 teaspoon baking soda
1 teaspoon ground cinnamon
1 teaspoon ground nutmeg
1 teaspoon ground allspice
1 teaspoon ground cloves
1 teaspoon ground ginger
1/2 cup chopped nuts (optional)

Four Kachinas Inn

Often you learn more about an inn and an innkeeper by listening to how they describe a recipe, "The *Pumpkin Bread* recipe originated with my friend Jeanette, one of the finest cooks I know. Jeanette and her husband began staying at the Four Kachinas Inn the first summer we opened. Even though I misunderstood the recipe and used canned pumpkin puree, instead of pumpkin pie mix, I loved the results and so did our guests." This recipe, by the way, won a Second Place ribbon at the Santa Fe County Fair—congratulations to the Four Kachinas Inn!

In a small bowl, soak the raisins in warm water to cover for 1 hour. Drain and set aside.

Preheat oven to 325° F. In a large bowl, mix together the oil, eggs, and pumpkin. In a separate bowl, combine the sugar, flour, baking soda, and spices. Add the reserved raisins and the nuts to the flour mixture. Add the flour mixture to the pumpkin mixture and blend together well.

Pour the batter into four small, greased and floured loaf pans and bake for 45 minutes, or until a tester inserted in the center of each loaf comes out clean. Let cool in the pans for 10 to 15 minutes. Remove from pans and let cool completely on a wire rack. Serve.

YIELD: 4 SMALL LOAVES

FOUR KACHINAS INN
SANTA FE, NEW MEXICO

Spoon Bread

1 cup white cornmeal
2 tablespoons butter
3 cups milk
3 eggs, well beaten
1 1/2 teaspoons salt
3 teaspoons baking powder

Preheat oven to 450° F. In a large saucepan, combine the cornmeal, butter, and 2 cups of the milk and slowly bring just to a boil, stirring constantly. In a small bowl, mix together the eggs, salt, and remaining milk. Add the egg mixture to the hot corn-meal mixture and mix until well combined. Stir in the baking powder.

Pour the batter into a greased 1 1/2- to 2-quart casserole dish and bake for 25 to 35 minutes, or until a tester inserted in the center comes out clean. Serve hot with butter.

YIELD: 6 TO 8 SERVINGS

THE CHALFONTE
CAPE MAY, NEW JERSEY

Maple Pecan Scones

3 cups all-purpose flour
1 1/2 tablespoons baking powder
3/4 teaspoon salt
3/4 cup (1 1/2 sticks) unsalted butter, chilled and cut into 12 pieces
1 cup chopped pecans
1/3 cup milk
2/3 cup pure maple syrup
2 tablespoons pure maple syrup

Preheat oven to 350° F. In a large bowl, sift together the flour, baking powder, and salt. Cut in the butter with a pastry blender. Gently fold in the pecans.

In a small bowl, whisk together the milk and the 2/3 cup syrup. Pour the milk mixture over the flour mixture and mix lightly until combined.

Roll out the dough on a lightly floured surface to a 1 1/2-inch thickness and cut out the scones with a 3-inch round cutter. Place the scones on a greased and floured baking sheet and brush the tops with the 2 tablespoons syrup. Bake for 15 to 20 minutes or until golden. Let cool on a wire rack or serve warm.

YIELD: 12 SCONES

RICHMOND HILL INN
ASHEVILLE, NORTH CAROLINA

Diane's Royal Scones

1 1/2 cups plus 2 tablespoons all-purpose flour
6 tablespoons granulated sugar
1 1/4 teaspoons baking powder
1/4 teaspoon baking soda
1/2 teaspoon salt
6 tablespoons firm butter
6 tablespoons currants, soaked in liqueur (any type)
1/2 cup buttermilk
Heavy cream
Ground cinnamon
Granulated sugar

In a large bowl, mix together the flour, sugar, baking powder, baking soda, and salt until thoroughly blended. Cut in the butter with a pastry blender until the mixture resembles cornmeal.

Preheat oven to 425° F. Drain the currants and stir the currants into the flour mixture. Make a well in the center of the flour mixture and add the buttermilk. Stir with a fork until the mixture pulls away from the bowl.

Gather the dough into a ball and pat into a 3/4-inch thick circle on a lightly floured surface. Cut out the scones with cookie cutters and place the scones 1 1/2 inches apart on lightly greased baking sheets. Brush the tops of the scones with the cream and sprinkle with the cinnamon and sugar. Bake for 12 minutes or until lightly brown. Serve warm.

YIELD: 18 SCONES

CASTLE MARNE
DENVER, COLORADO

Mary's Sticky Buns

1 cup warm water (105° to 115°F)
1 package active dry yeast
Pinch granulated sugar
3 medium potatoes, peeled and
  coarsely chopped
2^1/$_2$ to 3 cups water
1^1/$_3$ cups butter
1^1/$_2$ cups granulated sugar
1 tablespoon salt
4 eggs, beaten
9 cups all-purpose flour
Brown sugar
Slivers of butter
Ground cinnamon

Topping:

2^1/$_2$ tablespoons butter
1^1/$_2$ cups packed brown sugar
^{1}/$_2$ tablespoon dark corn syrup
Walnut halves

Manor House

Here it is! The most often requested recipe from the "Inn Country USA" series this past year was *Mary's Sticky Buns* from the Manor House. You will find out why once you bake your first batch. This is an inn with a sense of humor and the hospitality to match.

In a small bowl, combine the 1 cup water and the yeast and stir well. Add the pinch sugar and set aside.

In a medium-sized saucepan, cook the potatoes in the 2^1/$_2$ to 3 cups water for 10 to 15 minutes or until tender. Drain and reserve 2 cups of the cooking water. In a large bowl, combine the butter, sugar, and salt and mix in the reserved hot potato water. Mash the cooked potatoes and add to the bowl. Stir in the reserved yeast mixture and the eggs and blend well. Gradually add the flour, a little at a time, and stir until the mixture is doughy.

Turn the dough out onto a lightly floured surface and knead well. Place the dough in a covered container and refrigerate overnight to rise.

To make the topping: In a small saucepan, melt the butter, sugar, and corn syrup on low heat. Spread the mixture across the bottom of a round baking dish and sprinkle with the walnuts.

Roll out the chilled dough on a lightly floured surface. Sprinkle the brown sugar over the top and dot with the slivers of butter. Sprinkle the cinnamon over all. Roll up the dough jelly-roll fashion and cut into 8 equal pieces. Place the pieces into the prepared baking dish and refrigerate for at least 20 minutes.

Preheat oven to 375° F. Remove the chilled buns and bake for 20 to 25 minutes. Let cool on a wire rack or serve warm.

YIELD: 8 BUNS

MANOR HOUSE
CAPE MAY, NEW JERSEY

Potato-Cinnamon Buns

1 large potato, peeled, cooked, and
  mashed
1 cup milk
¼ cup (½ stick) butter, melted
¼ cup granulated sugar
½ teaspoon salt
1 package active dry yeast
1 tablespoon granulated sugar
¼ cup warm water (110°F)
4½ to 5 cups all-purpose flour
1 egg, beaten
1 teaspoon pure vanilla extract
Melted butter
Raisins (optional)
1 recipe Glaze (see recipe below)

Filling:
½ cup firmly packed brown sugar
¼ cup granulated sugar
3 teaspoons ground cinnamon

In a large saucepan, combine the mashed potato, milk, the ¼ cup melted butter, ¼ cup sugar, and the salt. Heat on low heat, stirring frequently, until lukewarm (110°).

In a large bowl, dissolve the yeast and the 1 tablespoon sugar in the warm water. Let stand until bubbly. Add the warm potato mixture, 2 cups of the flour, the egg and vanilla and beat un-til smooth and well blended. Slowly stir in 2 cups more of the flour.

Turn the dough out onto a lightly floured surface and knead for 10 to 15 minutes or until smooth and elastic. Add remaining flour as needed to prevent sticking. Place the dough in an oiled bowl, turning once to coat with the oil. Cover with a towel and let rise in a warm place until doubled, about 1 to 1 hour 15 minutes.

To make the filling: In a small bowl, stir together all of the ingredients and set aside.

Punch down the dough and knead just to expel air. Roll out the dough to a 15 x 18-inch rectangle. Brush with some melted butter and sprinkle with the reserved filling and raisins. Starting at the wide end, roll up the dough jelly-roll fashion and pinch the seam to seal shut. Cut the roll into 12 equal pieces and place the pieces, cut side up, in a greased 9 x 13-inch baking pan. Cover with a towel and let rise in a warm place until almost doubled.

Preheat oven to 375° F. Bake for 15 to 20 minutes or until richly browned. Let cool in the pan for 5 minutes. Re-move from the pan and let cool completely on a wire rack. Drizzle the *Glaze* over the cooled buns and serve.

YIELD: 12 BUNS

Glaze

$^1/_2$ *heaping cup confectioners' sugar*
2 tablespoons melted butter
$^1/_2$ *teaspoon pure vanilla extract*
1 to 2 tablespoons hot water

In a small bowl, combine the sugar, butter, and vanilla and stir until completely smooth. Slowly add the water to achieve a consistency that will drizzle over the cooled buns.

FOUR KACHINAS INN
SANTA FE, NEW MEXICO

Yeast Biscuits

1 package active dry yeast
2 tablespoons lukewarm water
2 cups sifted self-rising flour
2 tablespoons granulated sugar
$1/4$ teaspoon baking soda
$1/2$ cup vegetable shortening
$3/4$ cup buttermilk

Preheat oven to 450° F. In a small bowl, dissolve the yeast in the water. Let stand for 5 minutes.

In a medium-sized bowl, stir together the flour, sugar, and baking soda. Cut in the shortening with a pastry blender. In a small bowl, combine the dissolved yeast and the buttermilk. Add the buttermilk mixture to the flour mixture, a little at a time, stirring with a fork.

Turn the dough out onto a lightly floured surface and knead several times. Roll out the dough to a $1/2$-inch thickness and cut out the biscuits with a biscuit cutter. Place the biscuits on an ungreased baking sheet and bake for 10 to 12 minutes.

Variation: If all-purpose flour is used, add $2 1/2$ teaspoons baking powder and 1 teaspoon salt.

YIELD: 12 TO 16 BISCUITS

Rosswood Plantation

We literally "found" the historic Rosswood Plantation on our way from Vicksburg to Natchez, Mississippi. A last minute schedule change gave us a few minutes to leave the beaten path, and we came upon one of the best preserved antebellum mansions in the South. Retired West Point professor and career military officer Walt Hylander and his wife operate historic Rosswood the way you and I operate our own home. In fact, Rosswood is their home! Expect the Hylander's *Yeast Biscuits* to become a staple in your kitchen.

ROSSWOOD PLANTATION
LORMAN, MISSISSIPPI

Cappuccino Muffins

6 tablespoons softened butter
1/4 cup granulated sugar
1/2 cup unsweetened cocoa powder
1 tablespoon freshly ground expresso
   coffee powder
1 tablespoon baking powder
1/2 teaspoon salt
Grated peel of 1/2 orange
1 cup sour cream
3/4 cup cake flour
1 1/4 cups all-purpose flour
2 eggs, beaten
1 cup half-and-half
6 ounces bittersweet chocolate,
   chopped
Ground expresso coffee powder
Granulated sugar
Orange marmalade

Preheat oven to 350° F. In a large bowl, cream the butter and the 1/4 cup sugar with an electric mixer. Add the next eleven ingredients, blending between each addition.

Oliver Loud's Inn/ Richardson's Canal House

If you have never relaxed alongside of the Erie Canal and savored the pace of travel on the historic waterway near Pittsford, New York, you are missing one of life's rare moments. At the Loud's Inn, once your VIP welcome tray arrives you will think you have dozed off and awakened in 1815, and the stagecoach awaits.

When the batter is the consistency of thick sour cream, use an ice-cream scoop to divide the batter into greased, large-cup muffin pans. Sprinkle each cup with more coffee powder and some sugar and bake for 20 to 25 minutes. Let cool on a wire rack or serve warm with the marmalade.

YIELD: 12 LARGE MUFFINS

OLIVER LOUD'S INN/RICHARDSON'S CANAL HOUSE
PITTSFORD, NEW YORK

Lemony Orange Muffins

1 cup granulated sugar
²/₃ cup vegetable shortening
2 eggs, slightly beaten
2 tablespoons fresh lemon juice
3 cups sifted all-purpose flour
3 teaspoons baking powder
¹/₂ teaspoon salt
1 teaspoon ground nutmeg
1 cup milk
1 recipe Orange Glaze
   (see recipe below)
1 recipe Orange Butter
   (see recipe below)

Preheat oven to 350° F. In a large bowl, cream the sugar, shortening, eggs, and lemon juice. In a separate bowl, sift together the flour, baking powder, salt, and nutmeg. Add the flour mixture to the creamed mixture, alternately with the milk, beating well after each addition.

Fill greased muffin cups ²/₃ full and bake for 20 to 25 minutes. Remove and brush the warm baked muffins with the *Orange Glaze.* Serve with the chilled *Orange Butter.*

YIELD: 24 MUFFINS

Queen Anne Bed & Breakfast Inn

This lovely inn is really a pair of splendid side by side Victorians, originally constructed in 1879 and 1886. They are within easy walking distance of the Capitol building, the U.S. Mint, and the Denver Convention Center. You do not have to leave the inn, however, to enjoy some of the finest muffins in Colorado. Try these lemony taste sensations!

Orange Glaze

1 ¹/₂ cups confectioners' sugar
4 tablespoons fresh orange juice
2 tablespoons grated orange peel

In a small bowl, stir together all of the ingredients until well blended. Makes 1 ¹/₂ cups.

Orange Butter

3 tablespoons confectioners' sugar

2 tablespoons grated orange peel
1/2 cup (1 stick) softened unsalted
   butter

In a small bowl, mix together all of the ingredients until well blended. Chill. Makes 1/2 cup.

QUEEN ANNE BED & BREAKFAST INN
DENVER, COLORADO

Piña Colada Muffins

One 1-pound box yellow or butter
  cake mix
1 teaspoon pure coconut extract
1 teaspoon pure rum extract
1 cup flaked coconut
$\frac{1}{2}$ to 1 cup chopped nuts
One 8-ounce can crushed pineapple
  with liquid

Preheat oven to 350° F. Prepare the cake batter according to package directions. Add the remaining ingredients to the batter and mix for 1 minute. (Do not overmix.)

> ## The Magnolia Plantation Bed & Breakfast Inn
>
> Joe and Cindy Montaldo are in love with a Second Empire-style building in Gainesville, Florida, called The Magnolia Plantation. From the carefully landscaped tropical pond behind the inn to the hand-laid fireplace tiles, this place invites you to relax and enjoy. Definitely try Cindy's very popular *Piña Colada Muffins*.

Fill greased muffin cups $\frac{3}{4}$ full and bake for 15 to 20 minutes or until golden. Let cool on wire racks. Serve.

YIELD: 24 MUFFINS

THE MAGNOLIA PLANTATION BED & BREAKFAST INN
GAINESVILLE, FLORIDA

Mary's Pumpkin-Apple Streusel Muffins

2 1/2 cups all-purpose flour
2 cups granulated sugar
1 teaspoon pumpkin pie spice
1/2 teaspoon salt
1 teaspoon baking soda
2 eggs, beaten
1 cup canned pumpkin puree
1/2 cup vegetable oil
3 ounces cream cheese, softened
2 cups peeled chopped apples
1 recipe Streusel Topping
  (*see recipe below*)

Preheat oven to 375° F. In a medium-sized bowl, combine the flour, sugar, pumpkin pie spice, salt, and baking soda. In a large bowl, mix together the eggs, pumpkin, and oil. Add the flour mixture to egg mixture and stir together well. Mix in the cream cheese and blend well. Fold in the apples.

Fill paper-lined muffin cups 3/4 full and sprinkle on the *Streusel Topping*. Bake for 20 to 25 minutes. Let cool on wire racks. Serve.

YIELD: 15 TO 18 MUFFINS

White Lace Inn

Can you envision the color combination of rose, ivory, and raspberry? Those are the exterior colors of a little 1903 inn, nestled in a quiet old neighborhood in Sturgeon Bay, Wisconsin, called the White Lace Inn. Dennis and Bonnie Statz have done everything right here, including this recipe for *Mary's Pumpkin-Apple Streusel Muffins.* Enjoy!

Streusel Topping

1/2 cup all-purpose flour
1/2 cup granulated sugar
3 tablespoons butter, melted
1/2 teaspoon ground cinnamon

In a small bowl, mix together all of the ingredients. Makes 1 cup.

WHITE LACE INN
STURGEON BAY, WISCONSIN

Raspberry-Peach Muffins

1 cup diced fresh peaches
1/2 teaspoon ground cinnamon
2 cups all-purpose flour
1/4 cup granulated sugar
1/4 cup packed brown sugar
2 1/2 teaspoons baking powder
1/2 teaspoon salt
1 egg, beaten
1 cup milk
1/3 cup butter, melted
1 cup fresh raspberries

Sugartree Inn

Kathy and Frank Partsch think enough of their guests' creature comforts to ask in their Sugartree brochure, "Would you like a bottle of champagne awaiting your arrival, or a birthday cake, or perhaps an anniversary surprise?" With these gracious touches and special attention to detail, it is no wonder that this warm and inviting Vermont country inn has enjoyed so much success! Kathy says that they usually serve their *Raspberry-Peach Muffins* in the summer when the peaches are fresh, juicy, and abundant.

Preheat oven to 400° F. In a small bowl, mix together the peaches and cinnamon. Set aside.

In a large bowl, combine the flour, both sugars, baking powder, and salt. In a separate bowl, whisk together the egg, milk, and butter and stir in the reserved peach mixture. Mix the egg/peach mixture into the flour mixture until just moistened. (Do not overmix.) Gently fold in the raspberries.

Fill greased muffin cups 3/4 full and bake for 20 to 25 minutes or until golden brown. Let cool on a wire rack. Serve.

YIELD: 12 MUFFINS

SUGARTREE INN
WARREN, VERMONT

Applesauce-Granola Muffins

2 cups all-purpose flour
2 cups rolled oats
1 1/2 cups low-fat granola cereal
2 tablespoons baking powder
2 teaspoons salt
1/2 cup wheat germ
3 teaspoons ground cinnamon
1 cup granulated sugar
2 cups water
2 eggs, beaten
1/2 cup vegetable oil
3/4 cup unsweetened applesauce

Preheat oven to 400° F. In a large bowl, mix together the first eight ingredients. Stir in the water, eggs, oil, and applesauce until just moistened.

Fill greased muffin cups 2/3 full and bake for 20 to 30 minutes. Let cool on wire racks. Serve.

YIELD: 24 MUFFINS

LITTLE ST. SIMONS ISLAND INN
ST. SIMONS ISLAND, GEORGIA

Bran Muffins

1¼ cups whole wheat flour
1¼ cups all-purpose flour
2½ teaspoons baking soda
1 teaspoon salt
1½ cups granulated sugar
2 eggs, beaten
½ cup melted vegetable shortening
2 cups buttermilk
One 8-ounce can crushed pineapple, drained
1 cup diced walnuts
1 cup Raisin Bran cereal
6 tablespoons granulated sugar
2 tablespoons ground cinnamon
2 tablespoon melted butter

Preheat oven to 400° F. In a large bowl, combine the first five ingredients. In a medium-sized bowl, blend together the eggs, shortening, buttermilk, pineapple, and walnuts. Add the egg mixture to the flour mixture and blend well. Stir in the cereal.

Fill greased muffin cups ⅔ full. In a small bowl, mix together the 6 tablespoons sugar and the cinnamon and set aside. Spoon ½ teaspoon of the butter onto each muffin. Top with the reserved sugar mixture and bake for 15 to 20 minutes. Let cool on wire racks. Serve.

YIELD: 24 MUFFINS

VICTORIAN INN ON THE PARK
SAN FRANCISCO, CALIFORNIA

Chili-Cheese Corn Muffins

2 cups canned cream-style corn
2 cups yellow cornmeal
6 eggs
Salt to taste
1 teaspoon baking soda
2 tablespoons butter, melted
1 1/2 cups buttermilk
2/3 cup vegetable oil
1 1/2 cups grated sharp cheddar cheese
3/4 cup chopped canned green chilies

Preheat oven to 375° F. In a large bowl, combine the first seven ingredients and blend well. Stir in the oil, cheese, and chilies.

Fill sprayed muffin cups 2/3 full and bake for 30 minutes or until golden brown and firm. Let cool on wire racks. Serve.

YIELD: 18 MUFFINS

LITTLE ST. SIMONS ISLAND INN
ST. SIMONS ISLAND, GEORGIA

Corn-Blueberry Muffins

1 cup yellow cornmeal
¹/₃ cup granulated sugar
1 cup all-purpose flour
2¹/₂ teaspoons baking powder
¹/₄ teaspoon salt
1 cup buttermilk
6 tablespoons (³/₄ stick) unsalted butter, melted
1 egg, beaten
1¹/₂ cups fresh blueberries

Preheat oven to 400° F. In a large bowl, sift together the first five ingredients. Mix in the buttermilk, butter, and egg until just moistened. Gently fold in the blueberries.

Fill greased muffin cups ²/₃ full and bake for 20 to 25 minutes. Let cool on a wire rack. Serve.

YIELD: 12 MUFFINS

Simpson House
Santa Barbara, California

CHAPTER 6

Desserts

Apple-Cranberry Pie

4 cups peeled diced apples
Grated peel of 1 orange
Juice of 1 orange
¹/₂ cup cornstarch
³/₄ cup chopped fresh cranberries
³/₄ cup granulated sugar
One 9-inch unbaked pie shell

Topping:
¹/₄ cup (¹/₂ stick) butter
1 cup all-purpose flour
¹/₂ cup granulated sugar
¹/₂ teaspoon pure orange extract

Preheat oven to 375° F. In a large bowl, mix together well the first six ingredients and place the mixture in the pie shell.

To make the topping: In a medium-sized bowl, stir together all of the ingredients until sandy in texture. Spread the topping on top of the pie mixture and bake for 1 hour 15 minutes. Let cool on a wire rack. Serve.

YIELD: 6 TO 8 SERVINGS

Asa Ransom House
Clarence, New York

Lemon Frost Pie with Blueberry Sauce

2 egg whites
²/₃ cup granulated sugar
¹/₄ cup fresh lemon juice
1 tablespoon grated lemon peel
1 cup heavy cream, whipped
One 9-inch prebaked pie shell
1 recipe Blueberry Sauce
  (see recipe below)

In a large bowl, beat the egg whites and sugar with an electric mixer until thick and frothy. Slowly add the lemon juice and zest and beat until the mixture forms soft peaks. Fold in the whipped cream.

    Spread the mixture into the cooled, baked pie shell and chill. Serve with the *Blueberry Sauce.*

    YIELD: 6 TO 8 SERVINGS

Blueberry Sauce

²/₃ cup granulated sugar
1 tablespoon cornstarch
Pinch salt
²/₃ cup water
1 lemon peel, grated
2 cups fresh blueberries

In a medium-sized saucepan, combine the sugar, cornstarch, and salt and mix until completely blended and smooth. Add the water and lemon zest and cook, stirring constantly, until the mixture comes to a boil and is thick.

    Fold in the blueberries and return to a boil. Remove from heat and chill. Makes about 1 cup. (This sauce can be stored in the refrigerator.)

Variation: Raspberries, strawberries, or blackberries can be substituted for the blueberries. Puree the berries first, then push through a sieve to remove seeds.

THE FEARRINGTON HOUSE
PITTSBORO, NORTH CAROLINA

Frozen Peanut Butter Pie

1 recipe Chocolate Crunch Crust
   (see recipe below)
One 8-ounce package cream cheese,
   softened
One 14-ounce can sweetened con-
   densed milk
3/4 cup peanut butter
2 tablespoons fresh lemon juice
1 teaspoon pure vanilla extract
1 cup whipping cream, whipped
Chocolate fudge ice-cream topping

In a large bowl, beat the cream cheese until fluffy. Slowly mix in the milk until well combined. Add the peanut butter and mix until smooth. Stir in the lemon juice and vanilla. Fold in the whipped cream.

Pour the mixture into the chilled *Chocolate Crunch Crust* and drizzle the ice-cream topping over the pie. Freeze for 4 hours. Serve.

YIELD: 6 TO 8 SERVINGS

Chocolate Crunch Crust

1/3 cup margarine
One 6-ounce package semisweet
   chocolate chips
2 1/2 cups Rice Krispies cereal

In a small, heavy saucepan, melt the margarine and the chocolate chips on low heat. Remove from heat and gently stir in the cereal until completely coated.

Press the mixture on the bottom and sides of a buttered 9- or 10-inch pie pan and chill for 30 minutes.

THE BURN
NATCHEZ, MISSISSIPPI

Fruit Cobbler

8 cups fresh or frozen fruit
Granulated sugar (see box)
Water, fruit juice, or orange juice

Topping:
¹/₂ (1 stick) cup butter or margarine
1 cup granulated sugar
1 egg
1 teaspoon pure vanilla extract
1 cup unbleached all-purpose flour
¹/₂ teaspoon baking powder
Dash salt
Vanilla ice cream or whipped cream

Preheat oven to 375° F. Fill a 9 x 13-inch baking pan two-thirds full of the fruit. Sweeten to taste (see box). Add enough of the water or juice to come halfway to the top of the fruit. Set aside.

To make the topping: In a medium-sized bowl, cream the butter and sugar with an electric mixer. Add the egg, vanilla, flour, baking powder, and salt and beat until well blended. Drop by tablespoons on top of the reserved fruit and bake for about 45 minutes. Serve warm with the ice cream or whipped cream.

YIELD: 8 SERVINGS

> • *The amount of sugar depends on the tartness of the fruit.*
> • *Rhubarb, tart apples, and cherries require more than peaches or blueberries, but usually is not more than ¹/₂ cup of sugar.*
> • *When the fruit does not have enough juice, add the following: water with peaches, water and orange juice with blueberry, apple, strawberry, or rhubarb.*
> • *As the topping browns and forms a crust, break the top with the edge of a spoon to allow uncooked topping to come to the top and bake. Do several times during the baking period.*

MAST FARM INN
VALLE CRUCIS, NORTH CAROLINA

Spiced Blackberry & Cornmeal Cobbler

1 1/2 cups granulated sugar
1/4 cup packed brown sugar
1/2 tablespoon finely chopped lemon
  peel
1 teaspoon ground cinnamon
1 teaspoon ground nutmeg
1 1/2 tablespoons cornstarch
1 tablespoon dark rum
6 cups fresh blackberries
5 ounces (1 1/4 sticks) butter

1 1/2 cups confectioners' sugar
3 eggs, beaten
1/4 cup heavy cream
1 1/2 cups all-purpose flour
1 1/2 cups corn flour
1 cup cornmeal
1 tablespoon baking powder
3/4 teaspoon baking soda
1/2 teaspoon ground cloves
2 1/4 cups buttermilk

In a large bowl, combine the first seven ingredients. Fold in the blackberries and toss to coat. Place the mixture in a lightly greased baking pan and set aside.

In a large bowl, cream together the butter and confectioners' sugar. Add the eggs and cream and mix until well combined. In a separate bowl, combine both flours, the cornmeal, baking powder, baking soda, and cloves. Add the flour mixture to the butter mixture, alternating with the buttermilk, and mix together well.

Place the batter in a pastry bag with a straight tip and pipe the batter onto the reserved blackberries in a trellis pattern. Bake for 35 to 40 minutes, or until the crust is browned and the fruit is bubbly. Let cool on a wire rack or serve warm.

YIELD: 8 SERVINGS

INN AT BLACKBERRY FARM
WALLAND, TENNESSEE

Apple-Almond Tart

Crust:
1 ¼ *cups all-purpose flour*
½ *cup (1 stick) cold unsalted butter,*
  cut into pieces
2 *tablespoons granulated sugar*
1 *large egg, beaten*

Almond Mixture:
¾ *cup lightly roasted sliced*
  almonds

½ *cup granulated sugar*
2 *tablespoons unsalted butter*
1 *large egg*

Apple Mixture:
1 *large Granny Smith apple, peeled*
  and very thinly sliced
⅓ *cup apricot jam, heated and*
  strained
2 *tablespoons Triple Sec liqueur*

To make the crust: In a food processor, blend together the flour, butter, and sugar until the mixture resembles coarse meal. Add the egg and mix together until the mixture just forms a soft dough.

On a lightly floured surface, roll the dough out into an 11-inch round and carefully fit the round into a 9-inch tart pan with a removable fluted rim. Set aside.

Preheat oven to 375° F. To make the almond mixture: In the food processor, finely grind the almonds with the sugar. Add the butter and egg and blend until smooth. Spread the mixture evenly in the reserved crust.

To make the apple mixture: Arrange the apple slices on the almond mixture and bake for 25 to 30 minutes, or until the crust is golden. Let cool on a wire rack.

In a small bowl, whisk together the jam and liqueur and brush the glaze over the warm baked tart. Serve.

YIELD: 8 SERVINGS

CARTER HOUSE/HOTEL CARTER
EUREKA, CALIFORNIA

Venus de Phyllo

Pastry:
3 sheets phyllo pastry
¹/₄ cup melted butter
2 tablespoons granulated sugar
Confectioners' sugar

Filling:
¹/₂ cup whipped cream
2 tablespoons Frangelico liqueur
¹/₄ cup ricotta cheese
2 tablespoons confectioners' sugar

Sauce:
4 ounces dark chocolate
1 tablespoon butter
2 tablespoons Frangelico liqueur
2 tablespoons water

Garnish:
10 fresh strawberries, rinsed and
*   hulled*
2 tablespoons Frangelico liqueur
1¹/₂ teaspoons finely chopped fresh
*   apple mint*
1 ounce dark chocolate

Josephine's Bed & Breakfast

In our visits to inns across the nation over the past four or five years, I can truly state that we have never found an inn quite like Josephine's. It is definitely worth a visit to the sun-bleached community of Seaside, Florida. Josephine's talented young chef was so comfortable with our camera and crew, we wanted to pack him up and take him with us. His *Venus de Phyllo* is to die for!

Preheat oven to 375° F. To make the pastry: Place 1 sheet of the pastry on a dry surface. Brush with the butter and sprinkle with the granulated sugar. Repeat the procedure with a second and third sheet. With a cookie cutter, cut 12 shapes. Place the shapes on a parchment-lined, rimmed baking sheet and bake for 10 to 12 minutes. Let cool, then dust with the confectioners' sugar.

To make the filling: In a chilled bowl, mix together the cream and liqueur. In a separate bowl, mix together the cheese and sugar. Fold half of cheese mixture into the cream mixture, then fold in remaining half. Chill for 15 minutes.

To make the sauce: In the top of a double boiler, slowly melt the chocolate and butter over simmering water. Remove from heat. Stir in the liqueur and water and blend until smooth. Keep warm in a water bath.

To make the garnish: Quarter 2 strawberries and set aside. Slice the remaining strawberries and toss with the liqueur and apple mint. Chill. Shave the chocolate and set aside.

Fill a pastry bag with the chilled cheese mixture. On each dessert plate, pipe three rosettes about the size of a quarter at 11, 9, and 7 o'clock. Place a pastry shape on each rosette, angling it towards the center of the plate. Slide 3 to 4 slices of the marinated strawberries between the shapes and the rosettes.

Pour about 2 tablespoons of the warm chocolate sauce into the center of each plate and add a final rosette about the size of a half dollar in the 5 o'clock position. Garnish with the reserved strawberry quarters and shaved chocolate. Serve immediately.

YIELD: 4 SERVINGS

JOSEPHINE'S BED & BREAKFAST
SEASIDE, FLORIDA

Chef Juanita's Almond Tulips with White Chocolate Mousse & Raspberry Sauce

2 egg whites
¹/₂ cup granulated sugar
¹/₂ cup sliced blanched almonds
¹/₃ cup all-purpose flour
¹/₄ cup melted butter
1 ¹/₂ teaspoons pure vanilla extract
¹/₄ teaspoon pure almond extract
Dash salt
1 recipe White Chocolate Mousse
  (see recipe below)
1 recipe Raspberry Sauce
  (see recipe below)

Preheat oven to 350° F. In a medium-sized bowl, mix together the first eight ingredients. For each tulip, thinly spread 1 tablespoon of the batter onto a baking sheet and bake for 10 to 15 minutes. (Bake only two tulips at a time.)

Quickly remove the baked tulips and lay each on the bottom of a glass turned upside down. Place a large cup on the top of each tulip to mold. Let stand for 5 minutes, then remove the cup. Repeat the procedure with the remaining batter. Makes 14 tulips.

Fill the tulips with the *White Chocolate Mousse* and drizzle the *Raspberry Sauce* over the tops. Serve immediately.

YIELD: 4 TO 6 SERVINGS

White Chocolate Mousse

Three 6-ounce boxes white chocolate
  baking bars
4 cups whipped cream
Dash pure vanilla extract

Cut the chocolate into small pieces and melt in the top of a double boiler over simmering water. When melted, fold in the cream and vanilla.

Monmouth Plantation

Once in a great while we come across an inn that "has it all." In Natchez, a place where history and hospitality are inseparable, we discovered a resurrected 1818 mansion that is fast becoming a late twentieth-century innkeeping landmark. The Riches family has invested more than their love and dedication to Monmouth, and it shows in every detail. From the museum-quality antiques to the table settings fit for royalty, the Monmouth Plantation simply does not miss a beat.

Raspberry Sauce

*Two 10-ounce packages frozen
    raspberries, thawed*

*2 tablespoons fresh lemon juice
2 tablespoons kirsch liqueur*

In a blender or food processor, blend together all of the ingredients.

MONMOUTH PLANTATION
NATCHEZ, MISSISSIPPI

(Almost) Flourless Chocolate Cake with Raspberry Puree, Vanilla Ice Cream & Soft Cream

Cake:
2 pounds semisweet chocolate chips
1 1/4 cups (2 1/2 sticks) sweet butter
8 eggs, separated
2 tablespoons granulated sugar
2 tablespoons all-purpose flour
1/2 teaspoon salt
1 recipe Vanilla Ice Cream
    (see recipe below)
1 recipe Soft Cream
    (see recipe below)
1 recipe Raspberry Puree
    (see recipe below)
Unsweetened cocoa powder
Confectioners' sugar
Edible flower blossoms

Preheat oven to 400° F. Butter an 8-inch springform pan and line the bottom with parchment paper or wax paper. In the top of a double boiler, melt the chocolate over simmering water. Stir in the butter. In a small bowl, beat the egg yolks until thick and pale. Stir in the flour and add the egg yolk mixture to the chocolate mixture. Gently fold the egg whites into the chocolate mixture in three batches.

Pour the batter into the prepared pan and bake for 18 to 20 minutes, or until the center is set but not dry. Let cool for at least 2 hours.

Slice the cake into eight pieces. On each serving plate, place 1 slice of the cake, the *Vanilla Ice Cream*, and a dollop of the *Soft Cream*. "Paint" each plate with the *Raspberry Puree*. (Use a squeeze bottle). Dust one edge of each plate with the cocoa powder and the other edge with the confectioners' sugar. Garnish with the flowers and serve immediately.

YIELD: 8 SERVINGS

Vanilla Ice Cream

2 cups heavy cream
1 cup whole milk
1/2 cup granulated sugar
1 vanilla bean, split

In a medium-sized, heavy saucepan,

combine the cream, milk, sugar, and vanilla bean and scald the mixture over low heat until small bubbles begin to appear around the edge. (Do not scorch.)

Cover and refrigerate for 4 to 5 hours. When the flavor of the mixture is strong enough, strain the mixture and discard the vanilla bean. Pour the mixture into an ice-cream maker and freeze according to manufacturer's directions.

Soft Cream

1 cup heavy cream
1 tablespoon granulated sugar
1 teaspoon pure vanilla extract

In a small bowl, beat the cream with an electric mixer on medium speed until the cream thickens but does not peak. Add the sugar and vanilla and slowly beat to combine. Chill.

Raspberry Puree

2 cups fresh or thawed frozen raspberries
¼ cup Grand Marnier or Cointreau liqueur
1 tablespoon granulated sugar

In a blender or food processor, puree the raspberries until smooth. Add the liqueur and blend together. Add the sugar and blend until smooth. Strain the puree twice and set aside.

CARTER HOUSE/HOTEL CARTER
EUREKA, CALIFORNIA

Flourless Chocolate Cake with English Custard Sauce

Cake:

1 pound semisweet chocolate squares
1 cup (2 sticks) butter
9 eggs, separated
1 2/3 cups granulated sugar
2 teaspoons pure vanilla extract
1/4 cup Irish Cream liqueur

Custard Sauce:

9 egg yolks
1 1/3 cups granulated sugar
3 cups milk
1 tablespoon pure vanilla extract

Chesterfield Inn

Phil and Judy Hueber, the innkeepers of this delightful country inn, are very proud that their property has been serving people as a tavern, museum, farm, and inn since 1787. Now in its third century of hosting old and new friends, Chesterfield is the only inn in the "Inn Country USA" television series that walks their guests through the kitchen, rather than around it!

Preheat oven to 350° F. To make the cake: In the top of a double boiler, melt the chocolate and butter over simmering water. In a large bowl, whisk together the egg yolks and sugar for about 2 minutes. Add the vanilla and liqueur and set aside.

In a separate bowl, beat the egg whites until stiff peaks form. (Do not overbeat.) Fold the reserved egg yolk mixture into the chocolate, then gently fold in the egg whites and mix until well combined.

Pour the batter into a buttered 9-inch springform pan and bake for 40 to 45 minutes, or until a tester inserted in the center comes out clean. (The cake may appear sunken when baked.) Let cool on a wire rack.

To make the custard sauce: In the top of a double boiler, whisk together the egg yolks and sugar for 1 minute over simmering water. In a medium-sized saucepan, scald the milk. Add the hot milk to the egg mixture, whisking once, then slowly stirring with a plastic spatula, keeping the sides from hardening and the eggs from cooking. When thick enough to coat a spatula, remove the mixture from the heat. Stir in the vanilla and let cool to room temperature.

Ladle the custard sauce onto each dessert plate and place a slice of the cake on top. Serve immediately.

YIELD: 8 SERVINGS

CHESTERFIELD INN
WEST CHESTERFIELD, NEW HAMPSHIRE

Rum Cake with Crème Anglaise & Fresh Raspberries

Cake:

²/₃ cup butter or margarine

1 ³/₄ cups granulated sugar

2 eggs

1 ¹/₂ teaspoons pure vanilla extract

3 cups sifted all-purpose flour

2 ¹/₂ teaspoons baking powder

1 teaspoon salt

1 ¹/₄ cups milk

1 recipe Rum Sauce
(see recipe below)

1 recipe Crème Anglaise
(see recipe below)

Fresh raspberries

Preheat oven to 350° F. In a large bowl, cream the butter. Add the sugar and beat until light. Add the eggs and vanilla and beat until fluffy. In a separate bowl, sift together the flour, baking powder, and salt. Add the flour mixture to the egg mixture, alternately with the milk, and beat for 1 minute.

Spoon the batter into 6 greased bundt-style muffin cups and bake for 20 minutes, or until a tester inserted in the center comes out clean. Let cool slightly on a wire rack. Spoon the *Rum Sauce* over the tops of the cakes continually for about 1 hour.

Ladle the *Crème Anglaise* on each dessert plate. Place 1 cake in the center of each plate and drizzle more crème over each cake. Sprinkle on a few raspberries. Serve immediately.

YIELD: 6 SERVINGS

Rum Sauce

¹/₂ cup (1 stick) butter

1 cup granulated sugar

¹/₄ cup water

¹/₂ cup rum

In a small saucepan, melt the butter and stir in the sugar and water. Increase heat to high and cook, stirring constantly, for 5 minutes, or until the sugar is dissolved. Remove from heat and add the rum.

Crème Anglaise

2 cups half-and-half

3 egg yolks

¹/₄ cup granulated sugar

2 tablespoons Frangelico liqueur
¹/₄ teaspoon pure vanilla extract

In a medium-sized saucepan, heat the half-and-half until just before boiling. In a medium-sized bowl, beat the egg yolks and sugar with an electric mixer on high speed until the mixture is pale yellow and begins to thicken.

Reduce speed to low and slowly add the hot half-and-half in a steady stream. Return the mixture to the saucepan and cook on low heat, stirring constantly, until the mixture begins to thicken and coats a spoon. Remove from heat and stir in the liqueur and vanilla.

CASTLE MARNE
DENVER, COLORADO

Butter Almond Cake

2 eggs
1 cup granulated sugar
1 cup all-purpose flour
1 cup melted butter

Topping:
½ cup (1 stick) butter
½ cup granulated sugar
½ cup sliced almonds
1 tablespoon all-purpose flour
1 tablespoon milk
1 teaspoon pure almond extract

Preheat oven to 350° F. In a medium-sized bowl, beat together the eggs, sugar, flour, and butter with an electric mixer. Pour the batter into a greased 9 x 13-inch baking pan and bake for 20 to 30 minutes or until lightly browned on top.

To make the topping: In a small saucepan, melt the butter on medium heat and stir in the sugar. Add the almonds, flour, and milk, stirring constantly. Add the extract and continue to stir for 10 minutes or until thickened.

Pour the topping over the baked cake, then place the cake under the broiler until shiny brown and bubbly. (Watch carefully to prevent burning.) Let cool slightly on a wire rack. Cut into squares and serve warm.

YIELD: 8 TO 10 SERVINGS

MAINSTAY INN & COTTAGE
CAPE MAY, NEW JERSEY

French Tea Cakes

20 double graham crackers
¹/₂ cup chopped walnuts
¹/₂ cup (1 stick) butter
1 square baking chocolate
³/₄ cup granulated sugar
2 eggs, slightly beaten
Favorite butter icing

In a food processor, combine the graham crackers and walnuts and process until crushed and well ground. Place the mixture in a large bowl and set aside.

In a medium-sized saucepan, melt the butter and chocolate. Stir in the sugar and eggs and simmer, stirring constantly, for 1 minute. Pour the egg mixture over the reserved cracker mixture and mix together well.

Pat the mixture firmly into a 7 x 11-inch baking pan and frost with the icing. Chill for at least 1 hour. Serve.

YIELD: 8 SERVINGS

CASTLE MARNE
DENVER, COLORADO

Chocolate Mousse Cake with Two Sauces

*One 6-ounce package semisweet
  chocolate chips*
*One 6-ounce package milk chocolate
  chips*
½ cup (1 stick) butter
5 eggs
1½ cups granulated sugar
½ tablespoon cornstarch
½ tablespoon instant coffee powder
2 tablespoons whiskey
*1 recipe White Chocolate Sauce
  (see recipe below)*
*1 recipe Chocolate Sauce
  (see recipe below)*
Whipped cream
Chocolate curls

The Burn

When I asked Debbie and Larry Christiansen if they had any old photographs of The Burn dating back to the mid 1800s, they sheepishly offered a picture of Ulysses S. Grant standing on the steps of The Burn during the Civil War. These two innkeepers are not only masters of elegant understatement, but also are remarkably adept at assembling a staff of talented and attentive people. This *Chocolate Mousse Cake* recipe is one that I folded and pocketed before we left the kitchen!

Preheat oven to 350° F. In the top of a double boiler, melt all of the chocolate and the butter over simmering water. In a large bowl, beat together the eggs and sugar. In a small bowl, mix together the cornstarch and coffee powder and add to the egg mixture. Add the melted chocolate mixture and the whiskey to the egg mixture and mix together until well combined.

Pour the batter into an unbuttered 9 x 13-inch baking pan and place in the oven with a pan of water on the rack under the cake. Bake for 35 to 40 min-

utes or until set. Turn off the oven and let the cake cool in the oven.

Ladle 1 to 2 tablespoons of the *White Chocolate Sauce* on each dessert plate. Pipe concentric circles of the *Chocolate Sauce* over the top. Pull through these circles with a toothpick from the center to form a spiderweb.

Place 1 square of the cake on each plate to one side and garnish with the whipped cream and chocolate curls. Serve immediately.

YIELD: 8 SERVINGS

White Chocolate Sauce

4 ounces white chocolate
Heavy cream

In the top of a double boiler, melt the chocolate over simmering water. Add enough heavy cream to thin to the consistency of corn syrup. Let cool to room temperature.

Chocolate Sauce

2 ounces unsweetened chocolate

3 tablespoons water
3 tablespoons prepared coffee
$^1/_2$ cup granulated sugar
Pinch salt
3 teaspoons butter
$^1/_2$ teaspoon pure vanilla extract

In the top of a double boiler, melt the chocolate with the water and coffee over simmering water. Add the sugar and stir until dissolved. Remove from heat and stir in the salt, butter, and vanilla until smooth. Let cool to room temperature.

THE BURN
NATCHEZ, MISSISSIPPI

Walnut Torte with Chocolate Glaze & Apricot Puree

8 large eggs
³/₄ cup (1 ¹/₂ sticks) unsalted butter
4 cups roasted walnut pieces
1 ¹/₃ cups granulated sugar
²/₃ cup all-purpose flour
¹/₂ teaspoon baking powder
Pinch cream of tartar
1 recipe Chocolate Glaze
   (see recipe below)
1 recipe Apricot Puree
   (see recipe below)
Unsweetened cocoa powder
Whipped cream
8 fresh licorice mint or other mint
   leaves

Butter and flour a 10¹/₂-inch spring-form pan and line the bottom with parchment paper or wax paper. Separate six of the eggs and set aside. In a small saucepan, melt the butter and brown slightly. Set aside.

Preheat oven to 350° F. In a food processor, combine the walnuts and 4 tablespoons of the sugar and process until the walnuts are evenly ground but not oily. In a small bowl, sift together the flour and baking powder and set aside.

In a medium-sized bowl, beat the reserved 6 egg whites and the cream of tartar with an electric mixer on medium speed until foamy. Slowly add the remaining sugar and continue beating on medium speed until the mixture is stiff and glossy. In a separate bowl, mix together the ground walnuts, the 6 reserved egg yolks, and the 2 whole eggs. Pour the reserved butter over the mixture. Quickly fold in half of the beaten egg whites, then the reserved flour mixture. Quickly fold in the remaining egg whites.

Spoon the batter into the prepared pan and bake for 25 to 30 minutes, or until the cake feels springy to slight finger pressure and a tester inserted in the center comes out clean. Release the sides of the pan and let the cake cool on a wire rack.

Frost the cooled cake with the *Chocolate Glaze*. Place 1 slice of the cake on each of 8 large glass plates. "Paint" each plate liberally with the *Apricot Puree* and remaining glaze. (Use a squeeze bottle.) Dust each plate with the cocoa powder and garnish with the whipped cream and 1 mint leaf. Serve immediately.

YIELD: 8 SERVINGS

Chocolate Glaze

½ cup whipping cream
1 pound bittersweet or semisweet
  chocolate, chopped
4 tablespoons Rémy-Martin cognac

In a medium-sized, heavy saucepan, heat the cream to simmer. Add the chocolate and cognac and whisk until the chocolate melts and the mixture is smooth. Let cool for 10 to 15 minutes.

Apricot Puree

6 ounces dried apricots

¼ cup water
Juice of ½ lemon
½ cup Rémy-Martin cognac
¼ cup Grand Marnier liqueur
Juice of 1 orange
2 tablespoons white wine

In a nonreactive saucepan, combine the apricots, water, lemon juice and ¼ cup of the cognac and simmer on low heat until the apricots are soft and most of the liquid is absorbed.

In a food processor, puree the apricot mixture until fairly smooth. Add the remaining cognac, the liqueur, orange juice, and wine and puree again. (If the mixture is still not smooth enough, add more liquid.) Strain the mixture through a sieve and set aside.

CARTER HOUSE/HOTEL CARTER
EUREKA, CALIFORNIA

Chocolate Fudge Tart

1 pound 8 ounces milk chocolate
3 tablespoons butter
³/₄ cup milk
2 teaspoons pure vanilla extract
1 cup granulated sugar
3 eggs, beaten
2 cups chopped nuts
One 11-inch unbaked tart pastry shell

Preheat oven to 300° F. In a large, heavy saucepan, slowly melt the chocolate and butter with the milk. Add the vanilla and sugar and mix well. Stir in the eggs and nuts.

   Pour the batter into the tart shell and bake for 45 minutes. Let cool on a wire rack. Serve.

   YIELD: 8 SERVINGS

Asa Ransom House
Clarence, New York

Cranberry Crêpes

Batter:
3/4 cup all-purpose flour
1/4 teaspoon salt
1 1/4 cups milk
1 egg
1 egg yolk
1 tablespoon vegetable oil

Filling:
3 cups rinsed fresh cranberries
1 cup granulated sugar or to taste
1/4 cup all-purpose flour
1 cup fresh orange juice
1/4 cup citrus liqueur
1 1/2 teaspoons butter, divided
Sour cream

To make the batter: In a blender or food processor, combine all of the ingredients and blend together for 10 seconds. Let stand for 15 minutes.

Grease and heat a crêpe pan and a small skillet to medium-high heat. Spoon 2 tablespoons of the batter in the crêpe pan to cover the bottom. When the edges of the crêpe begin to brown, about 40 seconds, loosen the crêpe around the edges and invert into the heated skillet and cook until the other side is set. Repeat the procedure with the remaining batter. As each crêpe is prepared, stack and set aside. Makes 12 crêpes.

To make the filling: In a medium-sized saucepan, combine the cranberries, sugar, flour, and orange juice and cook, stirring frequently, until the mixture begins to thicken. Stir in the liqueur and cook for 5 minutes more.

Preheat oven to 325° F. Place 1 to 2 tablespoons of the warm berry mixture on each crêpe and fold the sides over. Place the filled crêpes in a greased 9 x 13-inch baking pan and dot each crêpe with 1/4 teaspoon of the butter. Bake for 10 minutes or until heated through.

Place 2 crêpes on each dessert plate and top with any remaining berry mixture and 1 dollop of the sour cream. Serve immediately.

YIELD: 6 SERVINGS

MANOR HOUSE
CAPE MAY, NEW JERSEY

Banana Crêpes with Raspberry Melba Sauce

1 recipe Raspberry Melba Sauce
(*see recipe below*)

Batter:
1¼ cups milk
1 egg
1 egg yolk
½ cup whole wheat flour
¼ cup all-purpose flour
Pinch salt
1 teaspoon vegetable oil

Banana Filling:
2 tablespoons butter
⅓ cup packed brown sugar
2 tablespoons tart orange or lime
  marmalade
4 to 6 firm ripe bananas, diced
¼ teaspoon pure almond extract
¼ teaspoon pure vanilla extract
¼ cup B and B liqueur
¼ teaspoon ground cinnamon

To make the batter: In a blender or food processor, combine all of the ingredients, except the oil, and blend together for 10 to 15 seconds.

In a crêpe pan, heat the oil on medium-high heat. Spoon 2 tablespoons

Briar Rose Bed & Breakfast

The secret ingredient in their highly acclaimed and award-winning *Banana Crêpes with Raspberry Melba Sauce* is the B and B liqueur. But the not so secret ingredient that makes the Briar Rose a "must visit" is the combination of the generous hospitality, the feather mattresses, and the crisp clean air of one of Colorado's signature cities.

of the batter into the hot pan to cover the bottom. Cook the crêpe for 40 seconds, then turn and cook until set. Repeat the procedure with the remaining batter. As each crêpe is prepared, stack and set aside. Makes 12 crêpes.

To make the filling: In a medium-sized skillet, combine the butter, sugar, and marmalade and heat until thoroughly melted and combined. Add the bananas and cook gently for 2 to 4 minutes. Stir in both extracts and liqueur and gently mix in the cinnamon.

Spread the *Raspberry Melba Sauce*

into the well of each dessert plate. Fill each crêpe with the banana mixture and roll up. Place 2 to 3 crêpes on top of the sauce and drizzle more sauce over the top. Serve immediately.

YIELD: 4 TO 6 SERVINGS

Raspberry Melba Sauce

12 ounces frozen raspberries, thawed
3 tablespoons granulated sugar
Juice of $^1/_2$ lemon

$^1/_4$ cup B and B liqueur
1 teaspoon cornstarch dissolved in
  1 tablespoon cold water

In a blender or food processor, combine all of the ingredients, except the dissolved cornstarch, and blend for 10 to 15 seconds. Strain the mixture through a sieve into a medium-sized saucepan and slowly bring to a boil. Add the dissolved cornstarch, stirring constantly, until thickened. Cover and set aside.

BRIAR ROSE BED & BREAKFAST
BOULDER, COLORADO

Chocolate Strawberry Shortcake with Strawberry Sauce

2 cups all-purpose flour
2 teaspoons baking powder
¹/₄ cup unsweetened cocoa powder
¹/₃ cup granulated sugar
¹/₂ teaspoon baking soda
¹/₂ teaspoon salt
5 tablespoons cold unsalted butter
¹/₂ cup chocolate chips
³/₄ cup milk
1 recipe Strawberry Sauce
  (see recipe below)
1 recipe Whipped Cream
  (see recipe below)
Fresh mint leaves

The 1785 Inn

Elijah Dinsmore, a veteran of both the French and Indian War and the American Revolution would be quite proud of the evolution of his home, one of the oldest and finest structures in an area known for its proud history. The 1785 Inn carries forth the Dinsmore tradition of gracious hospitality and splendid food, such as one of the inn's most requested recipes, *Chocolate Strawberry Shortcake with Strawberry Sauce.*

Preheat oven to 450° F. In a food processor, combine the flour, baking powder, cocoa powder, sugar, baking soda, and salt. Add the butter and chocolate chips and process until crumbly. While processing, add the milk and process until the mixture is crumbly again, but will hold together when pinched with fingers.

Turn out the moistened dough onto a lightly floured surface and form into a ball. Flatten the dough into a circle to a 1-inch thickness. With a 2-inch round cutter, cut out 12 to 16 shortcakes and place on a baking sheet lined with parchment paper or wax paper. Bake for 13 minutes. Let cool slightly.

Ladle 2 tablespoons of the *Strawberry Sauce* in the well of each dessert plate. Place the bottom half of 2 shortcakes on the sauce in each plate. Cover with 4 tablespoons sauce, 2 tablespoons of the chilled *Whipped Cream,* and the top half of each shortcake. Ladle 4 more tablespoons sauce over the shortcakes and top with 2 tablespoons whipped cream. Garnish with the mint leaves and serve immediately.

YIELD: 6 TO 8 SERVINGS

Strawberry Sauce

*2 quarts fresh strawberries, rinsed
   and hulled whole*
2 cups granulated sugar
1/2 cup fresh orange juice
*2 quarts fresh strawberries, rinsed,
   hulled, and sliced*

In a food processor, puree the whole strawberries. Pour the puree into a large bowl and stir in the sugar and orange juice. Fold in the sliced strawberries.

Whipped Cream

2 cups heavy cream
1/2 cup confectioners' sugar
2 teaspoons pure vanilla extract

In a medium-sized bowl, whip the cream with an electric mixer on high speed. When the cream begins to thicken, beat in the sugar and vanilla. Chill.

THE 1785 INN
NORTH CONWAY, NEW HAMPSHIRE

Spectacular Strawberry Trifle

Two 5.1-ounce packages instant
  vanilla pudding
Three 14-ounce pound cakes
Strawberry jam
2 cups orange liqueur
3 pints fresh strawberries, rinsed,
  hulled, and halved
Two 3-ounce packages ladyfingers
  (24 ladyfingers), split
4 cups whipping cream
¼ cup confectioners' sugar
2 teaspoons pure vanilla extract
1 pint fresh strawberries, rinsed and
  hulled whole

The Queen Victoria

**Everything that Dane and Joan
Wells do at Cape May's Queen
Victoria, they do very well. Their**
Spectacular Strawberry Trifle **is a
terrific example of their attention
to detail.**

Prepare the pudding according to package directions and set aside. Slice 1 pound cake into 3 thin layers. Spread the jam liberally on each layer.

Arrange the layers in the bottom of a large trifle bowl, cutting pieces to fit the bottom. Pour ½ cup of the liqueur over the cake. Arrange one-third of the halved strawberries over the cake. Pour one-third of the reserved pudding over the halved strawberries. Spread the jam liberally in the split ladyfingers and place the sandwiched ladyfingers around the edge of the bowl so that 1 to 2 inches of the ladyfingers are above the rim of the bowl.

Repeat the procedure twice with the remaining pound cake, jam, liqueur, strawberry halves, and pudding. (This should fill the bowl to within 1-inch of the top of the ladyfingers.)

In a large bowl, whip the cream until almost stiff. Add the sugar and vanilla and continue to whip until stiff. Mound the whipped cream on top of the trifle and garnish with the whole strawberries. Serve immediately.

YIELD: VARIABLE SERVINGS

The Queen Victoria
Cape May, New Jersey

Chocolate Chip-Amaretto Cheesecake

2¹/₂ cups fine graham cracker crumbs
¹/₄ cup granulated sugar
¹/₂ teaspoon ground cinnamon
¹/₂ cup (1 stick) unsalted butter, melted
1 cup semisweet chocolate chips
Five 8-ounce packages cream cheese, softened
1³/₄ cups granulated sugar
¹/₄ cup all-purpose flour
1 teaspoon pure vanilla extract
6 large eggs
¹/₄ cup half-and-half
¹/₄ cup Amaretto liqueur

In a medium-sized bowl, stir together the crumbs, sugar, and cinnamon. Add the butter and mix until well combined. Press the mixture on the bottom and halfway up the sides of a 9¹/₂-inch springform pan. Chill.

Preheat oven to 275° F. In a food processor, finely chop the chocolate chips. In a large bowl, cream the cream cheese with an electric mixer until smooth. Add the 1³/₄ cups sugar, the flour, and vanilla and beat until well combined. Add the eggs, one at a time, beating well after each addition. Stir in the chopped chocolate, half-and-half, and liqueur.

Pour the batter into the chilled crust and bake in the center of the oven for 2 hours 30 minutes. Remove and let cool in the pan on a wire rack. Chill, covered, overnight.

Release the sides of the pan and place the cake on a serving plate. Serve at room temperature.

YIELD: 8 TO 10 SERVINGS

ADAMS EDGEWORTH INN
MONTEAGLE, TENNESSEE

Carved Pumpkin Cheesecake with Caramelized Pecans

One 4¹/₂- to 5-pound pumpkin
Six 8-ounces packages cream cheese,
  softened
2 cups granulated sugar
1 tablespoon pure vanilla extract
Ground cinnamon to taste
Ground nutmeg to taste
10 eggs, beaten
15 egg yolks, beaten
1 cup heavy cream
1 recipe Caramelized Pecans
  (see recipe below)

Carve out the pumpkin and remove the pumpkin meat. Discard the seeds and strings and coarsely chop the pumpkin meat. In a large pot, cook the pumpkin for 20 to 25 minutes or until tender and reduced. Mash the cooked pumpkin and weigh out 2 pounds.

In a large bowl, mix together the mashed pumpkin, cream cheese, and sugar with hands. Slowly stir in the remaining ingredients, except the pecans, until the mixture is smooth. Whip the mixture with a whisk for 1 minute.

Preheat oven to 325°F. Pour the mixture into the pumpkin shell and place the pumpkin on a heavy baking sheet. Bake for 2 hours, or until the center of the cheesecake is set. Let cool on a heavy wire rack. Chill overnight. Serve chilled or at room temperature with the *Caramelized Pecans*.

YIELD: 8 SERVINGS

Caramelized Pecans

1 teaspoon olive oil
1 cup granulated sugar
8 ounces pecan halves

Rub the oil on a small serving plate. In a sauté pan, melt the sugar with the pecans on low heat, stirring constantly, until the sugar melts and is lightly browned. Pour the mixture on the prepared plate and let cool.

BEAUFORT INN
BEAUFORT, SOUTH CAROLINA

Eggnog Cheesecake

Crust:

4 cups fine graham cracker crumbs

2 teaspoons ground cinnamon

6 tablespoons melted unsalted butter

Filling:

2 pounds 6 ounces cream cheese, softened

1 1/8 cups granulated sugar

1/4 teaspoon salt

3 large eggs

1 teaspoon ground nutmeg

1 3/4 cups sour cream

1 vanilla bean, split; reserve seeds

Preheat oven to 300° F. To make the crust: In a medium-sized bowl, mix together the crumbs and cinnamon. Add the butter and stir until well combined. Press the mixture on the bottom and up the sides of a 9-inch springform pan and bake for 10 minutes. Chill.

To make the filling: In a large bowl, beat the cream cheese with an electric mixer on medium speed for 2 minutes or until smooth. Slowly beat in the sugar and salt. Add the eggs, one at a time, beating well after each addition. Add the nutmeg. Add the vanilla seeds and mix well.

Spread the filling into the chilled crust. Place the cheesecake in the oven and place a baking pan of hot water on the oven rack below the cheesecake. Bake for 1 hour 20 minutes or until almost set and a tester inserted in the center comes out clean.

Remove and loosen the baked cheesecake from the edges of the pan by running a knife around the inside of the edge. Let cool in the pan for 30 minutes at room temperature. Chill in the pan for 6 to 8 hours or overnight. Serve chilled or at room temperature.

YIELD: 8 TO 10 SERVINGS

RICHMOND HILL INN
ASHEVILLE, NORTH CAROLINA

Linda's Famous Cheesecake

Crust:
3 cups fine graham cracker crumbs
6 tablespoons (³/₄ stick) butter, melted

Filling:
Five 8-ounce packages cream cheese,
  softened
1³/₄ cups granulated sugar
3 tablespoons all-purpose flour
1¹/₂ teaspoons grated lemon peel
1¹/₂ teaspoons grated orange peel
¹/₄ teaspoon pure vanilla extract
5 eggs
2 egg yolks
¹/₄ cup heavy cream
Fresh strawberries, rinsed, hulled,
  and sliced

To make the crust: In a medium-sized bowl, stir together the crumbs and butter until well combined. Spray a 10-inch springform pan with vegetable spray. Press the crumb mixture on the bottom and up the sides of the pan. Set aside.

Preheat oven to 500° F. To make the filling: In a large bowl, beat together the cream cheese, sugar, flour, citrus zests, and vanilla with an electric mixture on high speed until just blended. Add the eggs and egg yolks, one at a time, beating well after each addition. Add the cream and beat until well blended.

Pour the mixture into the reserved crust and bake for 10 minutes. Reduce temperature to 250° and bake for 50 to 60 minutes. Slightly shake the pan and if the center is puddinglike and fairly set, the cheesecake is done. (Do not overbake.) Let cool on a wire rack. Chill overnight.

Top with the strawberries and serve chilled or at room temperature.

YIELD: 8 TO 10 SERVINGS

SIMPSON HOUSE
SANTA BARBARA, CALIFORNIA

Classic Bread Pudding

4 eggs
¹/₂ cup granulated sugar
2 cups warm milk
¹/₂ teaspoon pure vanilla extract
4 to 5 slices bread, toasted and buttered
¹/₂ teaspoon ground nutmeg

Preheat oven to 350° F. In a large bowl, whisk together the eggs and sugar. Stir in the warm milk and the vanilla. Break the toast into pieces and soak in the milk mixture for at least 20 minutes. Sprinkle the nutmeg on the top and stir to combine.

Pour the mixture into a 2-quart casserole dish and place in a shallow pan of water. Bake for 30 or 45 minutes, or until the pudding has puffed. Remove and let stand for 5 minutes. Serve warm.

YIELD: 6 TO 8 SERVINGS

1842 INN
MACON, GEORGIA

Warm Creole Bread Pudding with B and B Custard Cream

2 eggs, beaten
³/₄ cup granulated sugar
3 cups milk
1 cup heavy cream
¹/₂ cup (1 stick) unsalted butter,
  melted
2 teaspoons pure vanilla extract
1 teaspoon pure almond extract
¹/₂ cup dried currants, dried apricots,
  or dried Queen Anne cherries
1 teaspoon freshly grated nutmeg or
  to taste
8 ounces stale French bread, cut into
  ¹/₂-inch slices
6 tablespoons B and B liqueur
1 recipe B and B Custard Cream
  (see recipe below)
Orange zest

In a medium-sized bowl, combine the eggs, sugar, milk, cream, butter, both extracts, fruit, and nutmeg and blend together well. In a shallow bowl, place the bread slices and pour the egg mixture over all. Let the bread soak for 30 minutes or until saturated.

In a lightly greased, 8-inch square baking pan, arrange the soaked bread slices in two layers. Pour any remaining liquid over the bread and drizzle the liqueur over the top. Cover and chill for at least 4 hours.

Preheat oven to 350° F. Bake the chilled bread for 45 minutes, or until the custard is set and the top is a light golden brown. While baking, occasionally push the bread down into the custard with the back of a spoon. Remove the baked custard and let stand for 5 minutes.

Ladle ¹/₄ cup of the *B and B Custard Cream* on each large dessert plate and top with one 4-inch square of the bread pudding. Drizzle a slight amount of the custard cream over each square of pudding and garnish with the orange zest. Serve immediately.

YIELD: 4 SERVINGS

B and B Custard Cream

2 cups milk
8 egg yolks, at room temperature
¹/₂ cup granulated sugar
3 tablespoons B and B liqueur

In a heavy saucepan, heat the milk on medium heat until bubbles appear.

In the top of a double boiler, whisk together the egg yolks and sugar until well combined and the mixture is light yellow. Slowly whisk in the hot milk. Place over boiling water and whisk for 15 minutes, or until the custard is thickened to the consistency of heavy cream and coats the back of a spoon. (Do not overcook.)

Strain the mixture through a fine mesh sieve into a bowl and gently stir in the liqueur. Keep covered with plastic wrap, pressed directly onto the surface of the custard.

CARTER HOUSE/HOTEL CARTER
EUREKA, CALIFORNIA

Bread Pudding with Whiskey Sauce

1 loaf French bread, cubed
4 cups milk
3 eggs, beaten
2 cups granulated sugar
1 cup raisins
1 tablespoon pure vanilla extract
¹/₄ cup (¹/₂ stick) butter, melted
1 recipe Whiskey Sauce
  (see recipe below)

Preheat oven to 325° F. Toast the bread cubes in the oven until lightly toasted. In a large bowl, combine the toasted bread cubes, milk, eggs, sugar, raisins, and vanilla and mix together well.

Pour the melted butter into a casserole dish and add the milk mixture. Bake for 40 to 45 minutes or until set. Remove the baked custard and let stand for 5 minutes. Serve warm, topped with the *Whiskey Sauce.*

YIELD: 8 SERVINGS

Whiskey Sauce

¹/₂ cup (1 stick) butter
¹/₂ to ³/₄ cup granulated sugar

Madewood Plantation House

Madewood Plantation brings more to the table! Call it tradition, history, or simply dedication to impeccable hospitality, this Greek Revival masterpiece, known as The Queen of the Bayou, will absolutely charm you. The old kitchen that you see in The Madewood Plantation episode of "Inn Country USA" is their actual kitchen. We shot the preparation of dinner in front of the cooking fireplace. We will never forget this place.

1 egg, beaten
Whiskey to taste

In a small saucepan, melt the butter. Stir in the sugar and cook, stirring constantly, until the sugar is dissolved. Add 2 teaspoons of the hot sugar mixture to the beaten egg and blend well. Add the egg mixture to the sugar mixture and mix together well. Stir in the whiskey.

MADEWOOD PLANTATION HOUSE
NAPOLEONVILLE, LOUISIANA

Bread Pudding

¹/₄ teaspoon ground cinnamon
¹/₄ teaspoon ground cloves
1 teaspoon ground allspice
1 teaspoon freshly ground nutmeg
2¹/₂ cups granulated sugar
1 cup chopped pecans
3 cups milk
1 cup heavy cream
1 cup melted butter
¹/₂ cup molasses
4 eggs, beaten
1 cup plumped raisins
1 tablespoon pure vanilla extract
5 to 6 cups cubed stale French bread
Sweet cream

Greyfield Inn

With two exceptions, the inns that we have visited and filmed for "Inn Country USA" can all be reached by car. Cumberland Island, the southernmost barrier island off the coast of Georgia, is so far south that the inn receives its mail at Fernandina Beach, Florida. Late afternoon oyster roasts and breathtaking sunsets set the stage for some of the finest seafood dishes and delectable desserts.

Preheat oven to 375° F. In a large bowl, mix together the first six ingredients. In a separate bowl, stir together the remaining ingredients, except the sweet cream. Add the milk mixture to the dry mixture and stir until well combined.

Pour the mixture into a 2¹/₂- to 3-quart casserole dish and bake for 35 to 45 minutes. Remove and let stand for 5 minutes. Serve warm with the sweet cream.

YIELD: 8 SERVINGS

GREYFIELD INN
CUMBERLAND ISLAND, GEORGIA

Souffléd Orange-Almond Custard

¹/₂ cup (1 stick) softened unsalted butter
1 ¹/₂ cups granulated sugar
6 eggs, separated and at room temperature
²/₃ cup fresh orange juice
²/₃ cup all-purpose flour
Grated peel of 3 oranges
¹/₂ cup sliced roasted almonds
1 ¹/₂ cups milk
1 ¹/₂ cups heavy cream
¹/₄ teaspoon salt

In a large bowl, cream together the butter and sugar with an electric mixer until light and fluffy. Add the egg yolks, one at a time, beating well after each addition. Blend in the orange juice, flour, orange zest, and almonds. Add the milk and cream and mix well.

Preheat oven to 350° F. In a separate bowl, beat together the egg whites and salt until soft peaks form. Fold the egg white mixture into the milk mixture.

Pour the mixture into a greased 9-inch cake pan. Set the pan into a larger baking pan and add hot water to fill halfway. Bake for 1 hour. Remove and let stand for 5 minutes. Serve warm.

YIELD: 8 SERVINGS

This recipe was created by chef Russell Stannard.

RABBIT HILL INN
LOWER WATERFORD, VERMONT

Pumpkin-Pecan Crème Brûlée with Pecan Tuiles

12 egg yolks, beaten
³/₄ cup granulated sugar
1 cup pumpkin puree
1 teaspoon ground cinnamon
1 teaspoon ground allspice
¹/₂ teaspoon ground cloves
¹/₂ teaspoon ground ginger
¹/₂ vanilla bean, split; reserve seeds
Grated peel and juice of 1 orange
2 cups heavy cream
¹/₂ cup granulated sugar
1 recipe Pecan Tuiles
(see recipe below)

In a large bowl, mix together the egg yolks, the ³/₄ cup sugar, pumpkin, spices, vanilla bean seeds, and orange zest and juice. In a large saucepan, heat the cream to scalding and stir in the egg mixture, a little at a time.

Preheat oven to 225° F. Ladle the mixture into 8 custard dishes. Place the dishes in a high-sided baking pan and add water to fill halfway. Bake for 1 hour, or until the custard is firm. (Do not let the custard brown on top.) Remove and let stand for 1 hour.

Sprinkle the ¹/₂ cup sugar evenly on top of the baked custards and place under the broiler until the sugar is caramelized. Serve immediately with the *Pecan Tuiles.*

YIELD: 8 SERVINGS

Pecan Tuiles

1¹/₂ cups (3 sticks) softened butter
1 pound confectioners' sugar
8 egg whites
1¹/₃ cups all-purpose flour
1 pound pecans, finely ground

In a large bowl, cream together the butter and sugar. Add the egg whites and mix together well. Add the flour and pecans and mix for 2 minutes. Chill for 1 hour.

Preheat oven to 325° F. Place dollops of the chilled mixture on a hot, greased baking sheet. Spread thinly and bake until light golden brown. Gently remove each tuile with a spatula and bend each over a rolling pin to shape. Makes 8 to 10 tuiles.

CLIFTON, THE COUNTRY INN
CHARLOTTESVILLE, VIRGINIA

Chocolate Mousse

6 ounces semisweet chocolate
6 eggs, separated
¹/₄ cup rum
Whipped cream

In the top of a double boiler, melt the chocolate over simmering water. In a metal bowl, whisk together the egg yolks and rum until frothy.

Fold in the melted chocolate. Whisk the egg whites into the chocolate mixture until well blended. Chill for at least 2 hours. Serve with the whipped cream.

YIELD: 8 SERVINGS

THE SWAG COUNTRY INN
WAYNESVILLE, NORTH CAROLINA

Peppermint Mousse in Chocolate Cups

2 cups heavy cream
1 teaspoon unflavored gelatin dissolved in 2 tablespoons water
1 teaspoon pure peppermint extract, or ¹/₄ cup green crème de menthe
¹/₂ cup confectioners' sugar
Six 2¹/₂- to 3-inch diameter commercial chocolate cups

In a large bowl, beat the cream until stiff peaks form. Slowly add the dissolved gelatin and stir together well. Add the peppermint extract and sugar and stir until well combined. Spoon the mousse into the chocolate cups and chill. Serve chilled.

YIELD: 6 SERVINGS

ASA RANSOM HOUSE
CLARENCE, NEW YORK

Chocolate Marble Terrine

9 ounces white chocolate, coarsely chopped
¹/₄ cup (¹/₂ stick) butter, cut into pieces
4 tablespoons whipping cream
2 teaspoons cognac brandy
6 ounces semisweet chocolate chips
3 tablespoons butter, cut into pieces
¹/₄ cup whipping cream
2 teaspoons Kahlua liqueur
2 egg whites
3 tablespoons granulated sugar

Line a 9 x 5-inch loaf pan with wax paper. In a medium-sized saucepan, melt the white chocolate and the ¹/₄ cup butter. In a small bowl, whip together the 4 tablespoons whipping cream and the brandy until stiff peaks form. Gently fold the whipped cream mixture into the white chocolate mixture and set aside.

In a small saucepan, melt the chocolate chips and the 3 tablespoons butter. In a small bowl, whip together the ¹/₄ cup whipping cream and the liqueur until stiff peaks form. Gently fold the whipped cream mixture into the chocolate chip mixture and set aside.

In a small bowl, whip together the egg whites and sugar until stiff peaks form.

Add two-thirds of the egg white mixture to the reserved white chocolate mixture. Add the remaining egg white mixture to the reserved chocolate chip mixture. Pour both blended mixtures into the prepared pan in order and chill for 4 hours. Slice and serve immediately.

YIELD: 8 SERVINGS

TARA—A COUNTRY INN
CLARK, PENNSYLVANIA

Bittersweet Chocolate Soufflés with White Chocolate & Rum Sauce

Granulated sugar
8 ounces semisweet chocolate, chopped
1 tablespoon unsalted butter
1 tablespoon all-purpose flour
1/2 cup milk
3 egg yolks
1 teaspoon pure vanilla extract
4 egg whites
1 teaspoon fresh lemon juice
1/4 cup granulated sugar
Confectioners' sugar
1 recipe White Chocolate & Rum
    Sauce (*see recipe below*)

The Newcastle Inn

The Newcastle Inn is located in a quiet corner of Maine's famous Midcoast. If the mental image of lighthouse-crowned peninsulas and quaint little fishing villages where things seldom change appeals to your inn-going sensibilities, this is the inn for you. When you grow tired of watching the ospreys and ducks and you have savored Chris Sprague's culinary inspiration *du jour*, get ready to sample the *Bittersweet Chocolate Soufflés with White Chocolate & Rum Sauce.*

Lightly butter eight 6-ounce ramekins. Dust well with the granulated sugar and set aside.

In the top of a covered double boiler, melt the chocolate over barely simmering water, stirring frequently until smooth. Remove the top pan of the double boiler from heat and set aside.

In a medium-sized saucepan, melt the butter on medium heat, then stir in the flour and cook for 1 to 2 minutes. Briskly whisk in the milk for 3 minutes. Remove from heat and whisk in the reserved chocolate until smooth. Whisk

in the egg yolks and vanilla and set aside.

Preheat oven to 375° F. In a medium-sized bowl, beat together the egg whites and lemon juice with an electric mixer on medium speed for 1 minute, or until soft peaks form. Slowly sprinkle the 1/4 cup granulated sugar on top and beat on high speed until the egg whites are stiff but not dry. Using a rubber spatula, gently fold one-fourth of the egg white mixture into the chocolate mixture to lighten, then fold in the remaining egg white mixture.

Spoon the mixture into the reserved ramekins and fill each ramekin to the top. Bake for 17 minutes or until puffed and slightly cracked. Remove and dust with the confectioners' sugar. Serve immediately with a small pitcher of the *White Chocolate & Rum Sauce* on the side.

YIELD: 8 SERVINGS

White Chocolate & Rum Sauce

6 ounces white chocolate, chopped
$^1/_3$ cup dark rum

In the top of a double boiler, melt the chocolate over simmering water. Whisk in the rum until well blended. Remove from heat and let cool to room temperature.

THE NEWCASTLE INN
NEWCASTLE, MAINE

Chocolate Brownie Soufflés

Melted unsalted butter
Granulated sugar
$^1/_2$ tablespoon unsalted butter
1 ounce semisweet chocolate
1 cup Bavarian Cream
  (*see recipe below*)
2 tablespoons unsweetened cocoa
  powder
2 tablespoons granulated sugar
3 eggs, separated
2 tablespoons chopped walnuts
  (optional)
4 fresh strawberries, rinsed

Blue Harbor House

There is an 1810 New England cape home nestled by the wayside in Camden, Maine, that considers blueberry pancakes incomplete without blueberry butter. So you can just imagine then what they do with a supremely decadent dessert like *Chocolate Brownie Soufflés*. Enjoy!

With a pastry brush, coat four 4-ounce ramekins with the butter, then line each ramekin with the sugar. Chill.

In the top of a double boiler, melt the $^1/_2$ tablespoon butter and the chocolate over simmering water. In a large bowl, combine the melted chocolate mixture, *Bavarian Cream*, cocoa powder, and 1 tablepoon of the sugar and mix together until smooth and creamy. Mix in the egg yolks, one at a time. (If too thick, stir in a small amount of milk until light and creamy.) Stir in the walnuts.

Preheat oven to 450° F. In a large bowl, beat the egg whites with the remaining 1 tablespoon sugar until stiff. Gently fold in the chocolate mixture.

Spoon the mixture into the chilled ramekins until $^3/_4$ full. Bake for 8 to 12 minutes or until puffed. Remove and top each ramekin with the *Whipped Cream Topping* and garnish each with 1 strawberry. Serve immediately.

YIELD: 4 SERVINGS

Bavarian Cream

6 tablespoons granulated sugar
2 whole eggs
2 egg yolks
2 tablespoons cornstarch
2 cups milk

1 tablespoon pure vanilla extract or
   to taste
2 tablespoons unsalted butter, cut
   into ¹/₂-teaspoon pieces

In a medium-sized bowl, mix together
3 tablespoons of the sugar, the eggs,
egg yolks, and cornstarch and set aside.

In a 2-quart saucepan, scald the
milk with the remaining sugar and the
vanilla. Slowly stir the scalded milk
mixture into the reserved egg mixture.
Return the blended mixture to the
saucepan and cook on low heat until
desired thickness.

Remove from heat and return the
mixture to the bowl. Place the bowl in
a larger bowl with ice and beat the mixture until cool, adding the butter, one
piece at a time. (If needed, add cornstarch
to thicken.) Makes about 2¹/₂ cups.

Whipped Cream Topping

¹/₄ cup heavy cream
¹/₂ tablespoon granulated sugar
1 teaspoon rum

In a small bowl, whip the cream, gradually adding the sugar until stiff peaks
form. Gently fold in the rum. Makes
¹/₄ cup.

BLUE HARBOR HOUSE
CAMDEN, MAINE

Brandy Snaps

³/₄ cup all-purpose flour
²/₃ cup granulated sugar
Pinch salt
1 to 2 teaspoons ground ginger
¹/₂ cup molasses
¹/₂ cup (1 stick) butter
Brandy to taste (optional)

Preheat oven to 300° F. In a medium-sized bowl, sift together the flour, sugar, salt, and ginger and set aside.

In a medium-sized saucepan, heat the molasses to boiling. Add the butter and brandy, stirring to melt the butter. Remove from heat. Slowly add the reserved flour mixture and blend well.

Drop the mixture by 1 tablepoonful onto greased, unrimmed baking sheets and bake for 6 to 7 minutes. (The snaps will spread out and be very thin.) Remove and let cool slightly on the baking sheets. Remove with a metal spatula and place on wax paper to cool completely and harden. Serve. Makes about 50 snaps.

YIELD: VARIABLE SERVINGS

THE SWAG COUNTRY INN
WAYNESVILLE, NORTH CAROLINA

Snowballs

1 cup (2 sticks) butter or margarine, softened
$^1/_3$ cup granulated sugar
2 teaspoons water
2 teaspoons pure vanilla extract
2 cups sifted all-purpose flour
1 cup chopped pecans
Confectioners' sugar

Preheat oven to 325° F. In a large bowl, cream together the butter and granulated sugar. Stir in the water and vanilla and mix well. Blend in the flour and pecans until well combined.

Shape the mixture into balls. Place the balls on an ungreased rimmed baking sheet and bake for about 20 minutes. Remove from the baking sheet and let cool slightly. Roll the balls in the confectioner's sugar and serve.

YIELD: ABOUT 3 DOZEN

CASTLE MARNE
DENVER, COLORADO

Melissa's Shortbread

¹/₂ cup (1 stick) softened butter
¹/₂ cup granulated sugar
¹/₂ teaspoon pure vanilla extract
¹/₄ teaspoon pure almond extract
1 cup all-purpose flour
2 tablespoons cornstarch
Pinch salt

Preheat oven to 325° F. In a medium-sized bowl, cream the butter. Add the sugar and beat together until fluffy. Beat in both extracts. In a small bowl, sift together the flour, cornstarch, and salt. With a pastry blender, work the flour mixture into the creamed mixture until crumbly.

Gather the dough lightly together in a ball and place in an ungreased 10-inch tart pan with removable rim. With fingers, press the dough into a layer of uniform thickness. (The dough should be well pressed.)

With a thin knife, draw the dough slightly away from the edges and press the tines of a fork into the dough to decorate. Bake in the center of the oven for 40 minutes, or until the shortbread is a pale golden color and feels firm when touched lightly. (Do not let the shortbread turn brown.) Let cool slightly. Cut into small wedges and serve warm. Makes 16 wedges.

YIELD: VARIABLE SERVINGS

CASTLE MARNE
DENVER, COLORADO

Cornucopia

2 cups fresh red raspberries
1 recipe Crème Anglaise
  (see recipe below)
6 Italian waffle cones or cornucopia
3 cups fresh mixed berries, rinsed
  (blueberries, black raspberries,
  strawberries)
18 fresh mint leaves
Edible flower blossoms

In a blender or food processor, puree the raspberries. Ladle the *Crème Anglaise* into the well of each dessert plate and rotate to coat the well completely. Pipe the raspberry puree in concentric circles over the crème and run a toothpick in and out of the concentric circles.

Fill each waffle cone with the mixed berries and place on each plate. Garnish each plate with 3 mint leaves and decorate with the flowers. Serve immediately.

YIELD: 6 SERVINGS

Crème Anglaise

2 cups milk
1 teaspoon pure vanilla extract
4 egg yolks
3 tablespoons granulated sugar

In a medium-sized saucepan, heat the milk on medium heat just to boiling. In a medium-sized bowl, beat together the remaining ingredients with an electric mixer until begin to thicken. Add the hot milk very slowly on low speed.

Return the mixture to the saucepan and cook on low heat, stirring constantly, until begins to thicken. Remove from heat and set aside. Makes 2 cups.

Rose Inn

What do you get when you combine a world-class rose garden, an 1850 Italianate mansion, and two innkeepers—one who knows his way around the Black Forest and one who teaches other innkeepers how to artfully arrange table tops and plate presentations? Visit the Rose Inn and discover the answer.

ROSE INN
ITHACA, NEW YORK

Winter Fruit Poached in Port with Shortbread

1 recipe Shortbread (*see recipe below*)
3 cups tawny port wine
2 cups water
1 cup granulated sugar
2 tablespoons black peppercorns
1 stick cinnamon
1 cup halved dried figs
1 cup dried apricots
½ cup prunes
½ cup dried cherries
3 tablespoons pure vanilla extract
Favorite ice cream

In a large saucepan, combine the wine, water, sugar, peppercorns, and cinnamon stick and simmer for 20 minutes. Stir in all of the dried fruit and the vanilla and continue to simmer for 15 minutes, or until the fruit is tender.

Divide the warm fruit evenly on dessert plates. Place 1 wedge of the warm *Shortbread* on each plate and add 1 scoop of favorite ice cream. Serve immediately.

YIELD: 6 SERVINGS

The Lords Proprietors' Inn

At every turn, this inn and this town seem to beckon the traveler to come and rest. Sunsets highlight century-old Civil War cannons, while *Winter Fruit Poached in Port* awaits. We enjoyed ours with hand-churned ice cream!

Shortbread

1 cup all-purpose flour
¼ cup granulated sugar
½ teaspoon salt
1½ teaspoons baking powder
2 tablespoons unsalted butter
⅔ cup heavy cream

Preheat oven to 350° F. In a medium-sized bowl, combine all of the dry ingredients. Add the butter and mix together well. Stir in the cream.

Pour the batter into a greased baking pan and bake for 22 minutes or until lightly browned. Let cool slightly. Cut into wedges.

THE LORDS PROPRIETORS' INN
EDENTON, NORTH CAROLINA

Poached Pear Fans in Cranberry Sauce

4 firm pears, peeled, halved lengthwise, and cored
2 tablespoons fresh lime juice
2 cups fresh cranberries
1 cup apple juice
3 rounded tablespoons honey
½ teaspoon ground cinnamon
Pinch ground cloves
8 small sticks cinnamon
8 fresh mint leaves

Preheat oven to 350° F. Brush the pear halves with 1 tablespoon of the lime juice. Place the pear halves cut side down in a shallow glass baking pan and set aside.

In a 2-quart saucepan, combine the remaining lime juice, the cranberries, and apple juice and cook on medium heat until the cranberries pop and the sauce thickens slightly. Stir in the honey, cinnamon, and cloves until well blended.

Pour the sauce over the pears and bake, uncovered, for 30 to 40 minutes. (Pears should be tender but still hold their shape.) With a sharp knife, cut slits in the wider end of each baked pear half (do not cut through the top). Gently spread the slits apart to form a fan.

Spread 1 tablespoon of the sauce in the well of each dessert plate and carefully place 1 pear fan on top of the sauce. Place 1 cinnamon stick and 1 mint leaf in the top to create a "stem." Serve warm or chilled.

YIELD: 8 SERVINGS

THE LOVELANDER BED & BREAKFAST INN
LOVELAND, COLORADO

Spicy Poached Pears

2 cups cranberry juice
2 tablespoons granulated sugar
¹/₄ teaspoon ground cinnamon
Pinch ground cloves
1 teaspoon grated orange peel
¹/₂ teaspoon grated lemon peel
4 large ripe pears, peeled, halved lengthwise, and cored
8 fresh mint leaves
Fresh berries, rinsed

In a large saucepan, combine the first six ingredients and bring to a boil. Reduce heat to simmer and cook for 10 to 15 minutes. Place the pear halves in a baking pan, cover, and cook for 15 minutes.

   Place 1 baked pear half in each glass dessert plate and add 1 mint leaf where "stem" should be. Sprinkle each pear half with the berries and spoon 1 to 2 tablespoons of the sauce over each pear half. Serve warm or chilled.

   YIELD: 8 SERVINGS

OLD MONTEREY INN
MONTEREY, CALIFORNIA

Brandied Fruit Sauce

2 pints fresh strawberries, rinsed and hulled
2 pints fresh blueberries, rinsed
1 cup confectioners' sugar
2 shots brandy

In a medium-sized bowl, mash the fruit together with hands. Mix in the sugar and brandy and let stand for 1 hour.

Spoon the sauce over favorite pie, cake, or pudding 10 minutes before serving. Serve.

YIELD: 4 CUPS

The Greystone Inn

Maybe it is the champagne by the waterfall, or the afternoon cruise on pristine Lake Toxaway, or the hammock — whatever it is, this perennial favorite country inn in the western North Carolina mountains is the kind of place you really will write home about.

THE GREYSTONE INN
LAKE TOXAWAY, NORTH CAROLINA

Lemon Curd

4 egg yolks
1 egg white
¹/₄ cup (¹/₂ stick) butter
³/₄ cup granulated sugar
Grated peel and juice of 1 large
  lemon
Fresh fruit

Simpson House

Glyn's British heritage and Linda's artistic touches grace every quiet corner of this impeccably landscaped country inn in the heart of Santa Barbara. Imagine a string quartet on the lawn, quiet, bubbly fountains in the background, antiques galore, and a pair of innkeepers who have played leadership roles in preserving one of Santa Barbara's most historic homes—all this and perhaps the most comfortable featherbed you will find anywhere.

In a medium-sized bowl, combine the egg yolks and egg white and whisk together well. In the top of a double boiler, melt the butter over simmering water. Stir in the sugar and lemon zest and juice. Add the egg mixture to the butter mixture and blend together well. Cook slowly, stirring constantly, on low heat for 15 minutes or until thick.

Serve warm with the fruit. (The curd can be stored in a jar with a tight-fitting lid in the refrigerator for 2 weeks.)

YIELD: 4 CUPS

SIMPSON HOUSE
SANTA BARBARA, CALIFORNIA

Appendix

If you have enjoyed this fine collection of recipes from inns throughout the country, we encourage you to write or call the innkeepers with your thoughts and comments. Even better, visit the inns and get to know these gracious and friendly people.

Northeast

Asa Ransom House
10529 Main St. (Rt. 5)
Clarence, NY 14031-1684
tel: 716-759-2315
fax: 716-759-2791
Robert Lenz & Judy Lenz, Innkeepers

Blue Harbor House
67 Elm St., Camden, ME 04843
tel: 207-236-3196; 800-248-3196
fax: 207-236-6523
Jody Schmoll & Dennis Hayden, Innkeepers

The Chalfonte ✺
301 Howard St., Cape May, NJ 08204
tel: 609-884-8409
Anne LeDuc, Owner

Chesterfield Inn
Rt. 9, W. Chesterfield, NH 03466
tel: 603-256-3211; 800-365-5515
Judy & Phil Hueber, Innkeepers

The Darby Field Inn
PO Box D, Bald Hill
Conway, NH 03818
tel: 603-447-2181; 800-426-4147
fax: 603-447-5726
Marc & Maria Donaldson, Innkeepers

The Governor's Inn ✺
86 Main St., Ludlow, VT
tel: 802-228-8830; 800-468-3766
Charlie & Deedy Marble, Innkeepers

The Inn at Olde Berlin/Gabriel's
321 Market St.
New Berlin, PA 17855-0390
tel: 717-966-0321
fax: 717-966-9557
John & Nancy Showers, Innkeepers

Mainstay Inn & Cottage ✺
635 Columbia Ave.
Cape May, NJ 08204
tel: 609-884-8690
Tom & Sue Carroll, Innkeepers

Manchester Highlands Inn
PO Box 1754, Highland Ave.
Manchester Center, VT 05255
tel: 802-362-4565
fax: 802-362-4028
Robert & Patricia Eichorn,
Owners/Innkeepers

Manor House ✺
612 Hughes St.
Cape May, NJ 08204-2318
tel: 609-884-4710
Mary & Tom Snyder, Innkeepers

✺ *Designates inns that have their own cookbooks.*

The Mansakenning Carriage House
29 Ackert Hook Rd.
Rhinebeck, NY 12572
tel: 914-876-3500
Michelle & John Dremann, Innkeepers

The Newcastle Inn ❈
River Rd.
Newcastle, ME 04553
tel: 207-563-5685; 800-832-8669
Ted & Chris Sprague, Innkeepers

Oliver Loud's Inn/Richardson's Canal House
1474 Marsh Rd.
Pittsford, NY 14534
tel: 716-248-5200
fax: 716-248-9970
Vivienne Tellier, Innkeeper

The Queen Victoria ❈
102 Ocean St.
Cape May, NJ 08204
tel: 609-884-8702
Joan & Dane Wells, Innkeepers

Rabbit Hill Inn
Rt. 18, Lower Waterford, VT 05848
tel: 802-748-5168
fax: 802-748-8342
John & Maureen Magee, Innkeepers

The Red Lion Inn ❈
Main St., Stockbridge, MA 01262
tel: 413-298-5545
fax: 413-298-5130
Jack & Jane Fitzpatrick, Owners
C. Brooks Bradbury, Innkeeper

Rose Inn
PO Box 6576, Rt. 34 N.
Ithaca, NY 14851-6576
tel: 607-533-7905
fax: 607-533-7908
Charles & Sherry Roseman, Innkeepers

Sea Crest by the Sea
19 Tuttle Ave., Spring Lake, NJ 07762
tel: 908-449-9031
John & Carol Kirby, Innkeepers

The 1785 Inn
PO Box 1785
N. Conway, NH 03860
tel: 603-356-9025
fax: 603-356-6081
Charles & Rebecca Mallar, Innkeepers

The 1661 Inn/Hotel Manisses
Spring St.
Block Island, RE 02807
tel: 401-466-2421
fax: 401-466-2858
The Abrams Family, Innkeepers

Sugartree Inn
Sugarbush Access Rd.
Warren, VT 05674
tel: 802-583-3211
Kathy & Frank Partsch,
Owners/Innkeepers

Tara—A Country Inn
3665 Valley View, Box 475
Clark, PA 16113
tel: 412-962-3535; 800-782-2803
Jim & Donna Winner, Innkeepers

The Whitehall Inn
RD 2, Box 250, 1370 Pineville Rd.
New Hope, PA 18938
tel: 215-598-7945
Mike & Suella Wass, Innkeepers

Northcentral

Schumacher's New Prague Hotel ❋
212 W. Main St.
New Prague, MN 56071
tel: 612-758-2133
fax: 612-758-2400
Kathleen & John Schumacher, Innkeepers

White Lace Inn
16 N. 5th Ave.
Sturgeon Bay, WI 54235
tel: 414-743-1105
Dennis & Bonnie Statz, Innkeepers

Northwest

Romeo Inn
295 Idaho St., Ashland, OR 97520
tel: 503-488-0884
fax: 503-488-0817
Margaret & Bruce Halverson, Innkeepers

Turtleback Farm Inn
Rt. 1, Crow Valley Rd.
Box 650, Eastsound
Orcas Island, WA 98245
tel: 206-376-4914
William & Susan C. Fletcher, Innkeepers

Southeast

Adams Edgeworth Inn ❋
Monteagle Assembly
Monteagle, TN 37356
tel: 615-924-2669
fax: 615-924-3236
Wendy & David Adams, Innkeepers

Beaufort Inn
809 Port Republic St.
Beaufort, SC 29902
tel: 803-521-9000
fax: 803-521-9500
Debbie & Rusty Fielden, Innkeepers

Chalet Suzanne
3800 Chalet Suzanne Dr.
Lale Wales, FL 33853-7060
tel: 813-676-6011;
    800-433-6011
fax: 813-676-1814
The Hinshaw Family, Innkeepers

Clifton, The Country Inn
Rt. 13
Box 26
Charlottesville, VA 22901
tel: 804-971-1800
Craig & Donna Hartman, Innkeepers

Country Goose Inn
4957 Wooddale Ave.
Memphis, TN 38118
tel: 901-365-4766
Callie Pfannenstiel, Innkeeper

1842 Inn
PO Box 4746, 353 College St.
Macon, GA 31208
tel: 912-741-1842
Philip Jenkins, Innkeeper

The Fearrington House ❋
2000 Fearrington, Village Center
Pittsboro, NC 27312
tel: 919-542-2121
fax: 919-542-4202
Jenny & R.B. Fitch, Owners
Richard Delany, General Manager

The Gastonian
220 E. Gaston St., Savannah, GA 31401
tel: 912-232-2869; 800-322-6603
fax: 912-232-0710
Hugh & Roberta Lineberger, Innkeepers

Grandview Lodge
809 Valley View Circle
Waynesville, NC 28786-5350
tel: 800-255-7826
Stan & Linda Arnold, Innkeepers

Greyfield Inn
(Cumberland Island, GA)
PO Box 900
Fernandina Beach, FL 32035-0900
tel: 904-261-6408
Mitty & Mary Jo Ferguson, Innkeepers

The Greystone Inn
Greystone Lane
Lake Toxaway, NC 28747
tel: 704-966-4700; 800-824-5766
Tim & Boo Boo Lovelace, Innkeepers

Herlong Mansion
402 NE Cholokka Blvd.
Micanopy, FL 32667
tel: 904-466-3322
H.C. (Sonny) Howard Jr., Innkeeper

The Hidden Inn ❋
249 Caroline St.
Orange, VA 22960
tel: 703-672-3625; 800-841-1253
fax: 703-672-5029
Ray & Barbara Lonick, Innkeepers

High Meadows ❋
Route 20 S., Rt. 4, Box 6
Scottsville, VA 24590
tel: 804-286-2218; 800-232-1832
Peter Sushka & Mary Jae Abbitt, Innkeepers

Inn at Blackberry Farm
1471 W. Millers Cove Rd.
Walland, TN 37886
tel: 615-984-8166; 800-862-7610 (res.)
fax: 615-983-5708
Kreis B. Beall, Innkeeper

The Inn at Gristmill Square
PO Box 359
Warm Springs, VA 24484
tel: 703-839-2231
The McWilliams Family, Innkeepers

Josephine's Bed & Breakfast
PO Box 4767, Seaside, FL 32459
tel: 904-231-1940; 800-848-1840
fax: 904-231-2446
Judy, Jody & Bruce Albert & Sean Herbert,
Innkeepers

Little St. Simons Island Inn
PO Box 21078
St. Simons Island, GA 31522
tel: 912-638-7472
fax: 912-634-1811
Debbie McIntyre, Innkeeper

The Lords Proprietors' Inn ❊
300 N. Broad St., Edenton, NC 27932
tel: 800-348-8933
fax: 919-482-2432
Arch & Jane Edwards, Innkeepers

**The Magnolia Plantation
Bed & Breakfast Inn**
309 SE 7th St., Gainesville, FL 32601
tel: 904-375-6653
fax: 904-338-0303
Cindy & Joe Montalto, Innkeepers

Mast Farm Inn ❊
PO Box 704, Valle Crucis, NC 28691
tel: 704-963-5857
fax: 704-963-6404
Sibyl & Francis Pressly, Innkeepers

The Oaks Bed & Breakfast Inn
311 E. Main St.
Christiansburg, VA 24073
tel: 703-381-1500
Margaret & Tom Ray, Owners/Innkeepers

Prospect Hill Plantation Inn
Rt. 3 (Hwy. 613), Box 430
Trevilians, VA 23093
tel: 703-967-0844; 800-277-0844
fax: 703-967-0102
*Bill, Mireille & Michael Sheehan,
Innkeepers*

The Rhett House Inn ❊
1009 Craven St.
Beaufort, SC 29902
tel: 803-524-9030
fax: 803-524-1310
Steve & Marianne Harrison, Innkeepers

Richmond Hill Inn
87 Richmond Hill Dr.
Asheville, NC 28806
tel: 704-252-7313; 800-545-9238
fax: 704-252-8726
Susan Michel, Innkeeper

Silver Thatch Inn
3001 Hollymead Dr.
Charlottesville, VA 22901
tel: 804-978-4686
Rita & Vince Scoffone, Innkeepers

The Swag Country Inn
Hemphill Rd.
Rt. 2, Box 280A
Waynesville, NC 28786
tel: 704-926-0430; 704-926-3119
      212-570-2071 (off season)
fax: 704-926-2036
Deener Matthews, Innkeeper

Southcentral

The Burn
712 N. Union St.
Natchez, MS 39120
tel: 601-442-1344; 800-654-8859
fax: 601-445-0606
Larry & Debbie Christiansen, Innkeepers

Madewood Plantation House
4250 Hwy. 308
Napoleonville, LA 70390
tel: 504-569-7151
fax: 504-369-9848
Keith & Millie Marshall, Innkeepers
David D'Aunoy, Manager

Monmouth Plantation
36 Melrose Ave.
Natchez, MS 39120
tel: 601-442-5852; 800-828-4581
fax: 601-446-7762
Ron Riches, Owner
John Holyoak, Manger

Rosswood Plantation
Rt. 1, Box 6
Lorman, MS 39096
tel: 601-437-4215
fax: 601-437-6888
Walt Hylander, Owner

Southwest

Briar Rose Bed & Breakfast
2151 Arapahoe Ave.
Boulder, CO 80302
tel: 303-442-3007
Bob & Margaret Weisenbach, Innkeepers

Carter House/Hotel Carter
301 L St.
Eureka, CA 95501
tel: 707-444-8062; 800-404-1390
fax: 707-444-8062
Mark & Christi Carter, Innkeepers

Castle Marne
1572 Race St.
Denver, CO 80206
tel: 303-331-0621; 800-92-MARNE
fax: 303-331-0623
The Peiker Family, Innkeepers

Channel Road Inn
219 W. Channel Rd.
Santa Monica, CA 90402
tel: 310-459-1920
fax: 310-454-9920
Kathy Jensen & Susan Zolla, Innkeepers

Four Kachinas Inn
512 Webber St.
Santa Fe, NM 87501
tel: 505-982-2550
Andrew Beckerman & John Daw,
Innkeepers

The Gingerbread Mansion
PO Box 40, 400 Berding St.
Ferndale, CA 95536-0040
tel: 707-786-4000
Ken Torbert, Innkeeper

Hearthstone Inn ❈
506 N. Cascade Ave.
Colorado Springs, CO 80903
tel: 719-473-4413; 800-521-1885
fax: 719-473-1322
Dot Williams, Ruth Williams &
Mark Mitchell, Innkeepers

The Lovelander Bed & Breakfast Inn
217 W. 4th St., Loveland, CO 80537
tel: 303-669-0798
Marilyn & Bob Wiltgen, Innkeepers

Old Monterey Inn
500 Martin St., Monterey, CA 93940
tel: 408-375-8284; 800-350-2344
fax: 408-375-6730
Ann & Gene Swett, Innkeepers

Queen Anne Bed & Breakfast Inn
2147 Tremont Place
Denver, CO 80205
tel: 303-296-6666
Tom King, Innkeeper

Simpson House
121 E. Arrellaga St.
Santa Barbara, CA 93101
tel: 805-963-7067; 800-676-1280
fax: 805-564-4811
*Linda Davies, Glyn Davies &
Gillean Wilson, Innkeepers*

The Spencer House
1080 Haight St.
San Francisco, CA 94117
tel: 415-626-9205
fax: 415-626-9208
Jack & Barbara Chambers, Owners

Victorian Inn on the Park
301 Lyon St.
San Francisco, CA 94117
tel: 415-931-1830; 800-435-1967
Willie & Lisa Benau, Innkeepers

The White Swan/Petite Auberge
863 Bush St.
San Francisco, CA 94108
tel: 415-775-1755
fax: 415-775-5717
Celeste Lytle, Manager

Recipes Arranged by Inn

Sea Crest by the Sea
Featherbed Eggs, 30

The 1785 Inn
Chocolate Strawberry Shortcake with Strawberry Sauce, 190

The 1661 Inn/Hotel Manisses
Baked Herb Polenta with Fresh Concasse of Tomato, 94

Schumacher's New Prague Hotel
Vegetable Vomacka, 70
Mushrooms Kathleen, 60

Silver Thatch Inn
Chilled Apple Soup with Sorrel & Yogurt, 79
Yellow Tomato Soup with Fresh Thyme & Yogurt, 71
Grilled Salmon Crusted with Hazelnuts with Shiitake Mushroom, Pear & Applejack Compote, 132
Pan-Seared Lobster over Wilted Greens with Sweet Red Pepper-Mango Marmalade, 124

Simpson House
Lemon Curd, 218
Linda's Famous Cheesecake, 196
Yellow Gazpacho with Avocado, 78
Corn-Blueberry Muffins, 162

The Spencer House
Raised Waffles, 17
Dutch Babies, 14

Sugartree Inn
Raspberry-Peach Muffins, 158

The Swag Country Inn
Chocolate Mousse, 204
Brandy Snaps, 210

Tara — A Country Inn
Chocolate Marble Terrine, 205
Seafood Fettuccine, 128
Medallions of Beef Atlanta Bleu, 101

Turtleback Farm Inn
Ricotta Torte with Red Pepper Sauce, 32

Victorian Inn on the Park
Lemon Bread, 142
Spicy Buttermilk Coffee Cake, 41
Bran Muffins, 160

The Whitehall Inn
Vegetable Tulip Cups, 36

White Lace Inn
Mary's Pumpkin-Apple Streusel Muffins, 157

The White Swan/Petite Auberge
Mexican Eggs, 34

Note: We have endeavored to include the most often requested recipes from our "Inn Country USA" television series. If you see a recipe in an "Inn Country USA" episode that is not included in this cookbook, let us know. We will mail the recipe to you free of charge!

C. Vincent Shortt
Inn Country USA
205 Raintree Studios
Advance, NC 27006

Index

About the Author

C. Vincent Shortt is the founder and president of Shortt Stories Teleproductions, Inc., based in Winston-Salem, North Carolina. He has been a leading force in the hospitality industry and an award-winning producer of film and television programming for the past 20 years. He is an acknowledged authority on the food and beverage industry and a contributing editor and guest columnist for a variety of hospitality industry publications. Mr. Shortt is the only four-time recipient of the Pepsi MVP Award in the United States and has been honored by the National Restaurant Association with bronze, silver, and gold awards for menu design excellence.

Mr. Shortt is the executive producer of the PBS series "Inn Country USA." He is the author of the revised edition of *How to Open and Successfully Operate a Country Inn* and *The Innkeepers Collection Cookbook,* the first companion cookbook to his PBS series "Inn Country USA," both published by Berkshire House Publishers, Stockbridge, Massachusetts. He and his wife, Ann, live in Advance, North Carolina.